Praise for
Self Marketing Power

"Personal change usually precedes organizational change. That's why a book on self marketing is critical to building strong companies. Jeff Beals argues that employees have a moral obligation to use their gifts and talents—and the power of their personal brands—to help their companies do better. What would happen if everyone in your company made this choice?"

—**Drs. Kevin and Jackie Freiberg co-authors of** *BOOM! 7 Choices for Blowing the Doors Off Business-as-Usual* **and** *NUTS! Southwest Airlines' Crazy Recipe for Business and Personal Success.*

"How can one city produce an amazing money wizard like Warren Buffett and a leadership star like Jeff Beals? Maybe there's something in Omaha's water. Send me some...!"

—**Jay Lipe, author of** *Stand Out from the Crowd; Secrets to Crafting a Winning Company Identity* **and** *The Marketing Toolkit for Growing Businesses*

Believe. Project. Magnify. Advance. If Beals had filed a pre-flight plan for this book, then the preceding words would best describe the path taken in this quest to elucidate "personal branding." The author firmly believes that "You are a brand. You are a business of one." So the reader is driven to develop, maintain, and enhance a certain mindset. Every utterance, every appearance, every movement has to be exquisitely controlled to present a superior image, no matter how informal the circumstances or the sophistication of the audience. The title may have been alternatively named "self promotion." Both names, however, are misleading. Although one may not realize it until nearing the end chapters, the book is really about self-actualization, or achieving the pinnacle of professional capability.

—ForeWord Magazine

"Jeff's book is an essential tool for anyone in the business world today, regardless of their title or their role. Read his book, understand what he's talking about, and do what he suggests. You'll find only success for your efforts."

—**Cam Marston, speaker and author of** *Motivating the "What's In It For Me?" Workforce.*

"Jeff Beals has done an excellent job explaining the reality that "people are products". Whether deliberate or not, you create your own brand through your actions. What picture pops into someone's mind when they hear your name is totally within your control. Self Marketing Power is a manual for managing your personal brand."

—**Robert Gordman, author of** *The Must-Have Customer* **and** *Secrets of the $uper $weet $pot*

"Jeff's book is thoughtful, well written, and very practical. Self marketing that doesn't smack of blatant self promotion is critical to success. Self Marketing Power shows how to strike the right balance."

—**Jim Clemmer, practical leadership author, speaker, and workshop leader**

"In this great book, Jeff Beals manages to pull off an enormous feat by providing chapter after chapter of information that is valuable for anyone and everyone, no matter what stage they are at in their career. Clearly a man with abundant experience in the field, Beals provides his readers with everything that is important about self-marketing. He gives all of the information you need to know from how to develop a high level of name recognition to the power of a positive attitude to what to do in those awkward foot-in-mouth situations (My favorite chapter!) and does it in a way that both inspires and excites. A great read for anyone in business—experienced and inexperienced alike!"

—**Ty Freyvogel, author of** *It's Not Your Smarts, It's Your Schmooze: How to Succeed Without Being Brilliant* **and** *Seize the Century!*

"I have read Jeff's book, Self Marketing Power, and heard him speak on the same topic. His insights are dead-on. He clearly explains ways that one can achieve growth in his or her career by promoting himself without coming off as brash or self-absorbed. His successful real estate career, radio program, book, and speaking abilities show that he lives what he teaches."
—**David DeFord, author, speaker, trainer**

"Jeff Beals' Self Marketing Power offers a practical guide to personal branding that every business professional can use. We think the strategies in it are so comprehensive and powerful that we have decided to provide a copy of the book to each of our career transition clients."
—**Dan Weber and Gerry Phelan of Peak Pathways Executive Coaching**

"As the keynote speaker at our annual meeting, Jeff Beals held our franchise owners' interest and inspired them to take their business to the next level. Learning to market themselves as 'a brand of one' was the perfect message for them to take back home and include in their marketing plans."
—**Roland Bates, president, National Property Inspections, Inc.**

"Jeff Beals is a compelling speaker and author. His book Self-Marketing Power is a blueprint for success no matter what your title or field. His strategies for "becoming a celebrity in your own sphere of interest" not only help you become the go-to resource in your network, but is based not on cut-throat competition but on creating mutually beneficial relationships. If you've never heard him speak, make it a priority!"
—**Susan Baird, freelance writer**

SELF
MARKETING
POWER

Jeff Beals

Branding
Yourself as a
Business of One

Keynote Publishing • Omaha, NE

Library of Congress Control Number: 2007931587
ISBN-10: 0-9797438-0-X
ISBN-13: 978-0-9797438-0-1

Cataloging in Publication Data on file with Publisher

Cover and Interior Design © TLC Graphics, www.TLCGraphics.com
Editorial services: Sandra Wendel, Write-on Inc.
Marketing and Publicity: Concierge Marketing Inc.
Author photos: Blaser Photography, Omaha, NE

Keynote Publishing, LLC
PO Box 540663
Omaha, NE 68154
www.selfmarketingpower.com
Printed in the United States of America.

10 9 8 7 6 5 4 3 2

To My Son, Jack Robert Beals:

*May you achieve great success in your life -
however you choose to define it*

Preface

LTHOUGH THE TITLE OF THIS BOOK IS *SELF MARKETING POWER: Branding Yourself as a Business of One*, it is really much more than that. Above all, it is a book about success – personal, career and business success.

I wrote this book hoping to make a difference in the readers' lives. I want to help people be more successful and come closer to realizing the tremendous potential that dwells inside them. As a former college dean and current part-time collegiate instructor, I care a great deal about the success and personal fulfillment of those around me. Fostering success in others is simply part of my nature.

It is my belief that self marketing is an essential component of career success. Too often I have seen talented – but excessively modest – people work tirelessly only to watch someone else benefit in the end. Too often I have seen potentially successful people fall short of their goals, because they didn't know how to promote themselves in an assertive but tasteful manner.

Today's marketplace is crowded and noisy. That's why self marketing is so important. Billions of people are competing for the spotlight.

Those who actually get the spotlight to shine on them are the ones who flourish.

Whether you're hoping for a job promotion, trying to land a big client or striving to make a difference in your community, one thing is for sure: you have to stand out. You have to speak out on your behalf. Successful people must know and use the secrets of self marketing.

This book reveals and explains these self marketing secrets. It helps you, regardless of your current success level, go further down the path toward high-level self marketing competence – an almost magical realm where your self marketing is purposeful and directed but outwardly appears humble and effortless.

Self Marketing Power's content comes from diligent research and close observation of highly successful individuals as well as my personal experience as a real estate executive, academician, radio talk show host and newspaper columnist.

As you read on, you will quickly realize two of my most significant self marketing philosophies.

First, professionals in any industry are businesses unto themselves. Each person is a brand. Regardless of your chosen profession, you are a "business of one" rather than an employee of someone else's business.

Second, each professional needs to think like a politician. Like the politician running for office, you are campaigning for something. It's a personal, lifelong campaign for whatever matters to you. Politicians never miss an opportunity to promote themselves before potential voters. Likewise, you should constantly promote your brand to your own personal "voters."

The first four chapters of *Self Marketing Power* explain exactly what self marketing is and why ambitious professionals must engage in it. Chapters 5 through 12 discuss the nuts and bolts of self marketing: how you actually market yourself in an effective but tactful way.

Chapters 13 through 20 are critically important, because they explore how the traditional elements of success – attitudes, philosophies and behaviors – should be synthesized with self marketing principles.

PREFACE

Those readers who are interested in pursuing different career opportunities will be particularly interested in Chapter 17, which provides a new and refreshing approach to the job search process.

Self Marketing Power is written for anyone who wants more from life, but it is especially useful for:

- Ambitious people who want to move up
- Professionals who are feeling restless in their current jobs
- Salespersons hoping to do more business
- Business owners who want to boost revenue
- Prospective entrepreneurs who have not yet pulled the trigger
- Community volunteers who want to establish bigger names for themselves in order to make a bigger difference
- Recent college graduates who want to accelerate their career success

Upon completing this book, I hope you are left with new insight and practical, how-to knowledge, but I also hope you are left with a lot of "feelings." Among these feelings would be excitement, inspiration, confidence, enthusiasm and motivation.

By simply picking up this book, you probably possess the basic interest and desire to accomplish more and rise higher. The trick is to put that interest and desire to work for you. By doing so, you just may achieve the highest levels of career and life success you have ever imagined.

Acknowledgments

WRITING A BOOK IS A MAJOR UNDERTAKING AND REQUIRES THE SUPPORT of many people. Fortunately, there have been many by my side along the way.

The support of my family means everything to me. I would especially like to thank my wife, Stephanie Beals, who always provides me great support and encouragement. I am blessed, because she is a great wife, friend and business partner but also a wonderful, loving mom to our son, Jack.

I am indebted to my parents, Terry and Mary Beals, and several other family members including Dr. Greg and Maria Beals, Scott and Jill Graves, Kacie Beals, Rollie and Shirley Winter, Manish Das and Lisa Winter-Das.

My trusted friend and confidant, Trenton Magid, is my employer at Coldwell Banker Commercial World Group and my business partner in a couple other ventures. My long friendship with him has given me great material for this book, but just as valuable, his support and understanding gave me the confidence to pursue it.

Jim Vokal, another colleague at Coldwell Banker Commercial World Group, is a close friend and my next-door neighbor at the office. He has had to endure frequent updates about the progress of this book. His encouragement has been valuable. I would also like to thank Tucker Magid, Ryan Callinan, Jennifer Turkel, Carl Weiland, Carol Behm, Jean Lahti, Bob Robinson and the entire team at Coldwell Banker Commercial World Group. Elaine Clark, our Director of Accounting, played a major role in this effort a couple years ago, when she asked me to deliver a speech on self marketing for her chapter of American Society of Women Accountants.

As a man with many interests, I have several "part-time jobs" in addition to my full-time work in commercial real estate. My side jobs have given me the perspective necessary to understand self marketing and personal success more deeply. In that spirit, I am very appreciative of Dr. Lou Pol (Dean), Dr. Kim Sosin (Chairwoman Emeritus, Department of Economics), Dr. Roger Sindt (Director, Real Estate and Land Use Economics Program) and Dr. Donald Baum (Chairman, Department of Economics) of the University of Nebraska at Omaha College of Business Administration.

I would also like to acknowledge Gary Sadlemyer, Bill Ryan, Roger Olson, Scott Voorhees, Jim Rose, Tom Stanton, Ken Wurdeman, and the entire team at News Radio 1110 KFAB. I also appreciate and value my strong relationship with the guys at *The City Weekly* especially Jim Minge, Dan Beckman and Andy Ruback.

A significant portion of this book's content came from my work in student affairs and the career success presentations I have been giving to college students for 10 years. Accordingly, I am grateful to Patrick McBride, Dr. Terry Dixon, Estelle Johnson, Terri Heggemeyer, Jason Barelman, Connie Bottger, Dr. Theresa Lamsam, Heather Nelson, Pat Crisler, Jane Schaefer and Dr. Andrew Gustafson.

A book cannot be successful without a great publishing team. I received marvelous support and guidance from Lisa Pelto, owner of Concierge Marketing, who persistently encouraged me to turn my speeches and lectures on self marketing into this book. I also appreciate my editor, Sandra Wendel. TLC Graphics of Austin, Texas, designed the cover and interior of the book. A big thank you goes to my friend,

ACKNOWLEDGMENTS

Mitch Arnold, owner of Preferred Partners, who manages www.selfmarketingpower.com. He also handles the website for my radio program.

In preparing this book, several friends and professional acquaintances have been great at providing support and giving advice. In particular, I would like to mention Scott Kennedy, Kirk Swartzbaugh, Scharlie Fitts, Dave Arch, Kristine Gerber, Pete Coen, Darren Obrecht, April Kelly, Frank Allen, Karla Ewert, Lou Chiganos, Rob Krohn, Bridget Lynch, Michele Singh, Rev. Lou Forney, Scott Meyerson, Kurt Cimino, Jerry O'Doherty, Nicole Adams, Jason Butts, Craig Wolf, Juleen Olson, Jerry Wajda, Jennifer Wurth, Ammy Magid and George Morgan.

Contents

- Each of us has a personal brand.
- We need to promote ourselves in our careers just like a politician running for office.

- It is more "art" than science.
- Only a fine line separates self marketing from egotistical boasting.

- In a competitive, fast-moving, global economy, you must be noticed in order to succeed.

CONTENTS

13. Bend All the Rules: Creativity Is Key. 151
- You can market yourself by creating something unique and of value.
- Creativity elevates you above your competitors.
- Be the first. Be the only.

14. Never Stop Learning 159
- Learning is a lifelong endeavor.
- Only wise, talented and up-to-date people are effective self marketers.

15. From Ordinary to Extraordinary:
Planning, Goal Setting and Time Management. 169
- How to turn your dreams into reasonable action plans.
- Avoid the time traps that can bog down your self marketing as well as your whole career.

16. Make It Look Easy: Perpetual Professionalism 191
- Consistent behavior is essential.
- Assume you are always being watched; act accordingly.
- Have your printed, personal marketing pieces ready to go at all times.

17. From "Don't Know You" to "Can't Live Without You" 203
- How to get the upper hand in the job-search process.
- Empathizing with the hiring manager gives you an advantage over other candidates.
- How to prove you are the solution to the hiring manager's problem.

CONTENTS

Introduction

ARE YOU READY TO CHANGE YOUR FUTURE?

A LITTLE APPREHENSIVELY, I STEPPED TO THE PODIUM AND PEERED OUT AT the luncheon crowd. I was simultaneously nervous and excited. I had just become a volunteer speaker on behalf of a political campaign committee, and this was my first gig.

It was the spring of 2000, and a group of business and civic leaders in my hometown came together to persuade local voters that they should approve a $198-million bond issue in the upcoming election. The funds would go toward construction of a sports arena and convention center, something my city needed badly. I was such a big believer in the cause that I joined the campaign committee and logged hundreds of volunteer hours. Before I knew it, I was one of the spokesmen. I spoke to neighborhood groups, professional associations and just about any other organization that would listen to me.

The more I campaigned on behalf of the convention center, the more fascinated I became with the entire political process. It was fun and exciting. It was fast paced. It was an amazing social experience, giving me the opportunity to rub elbows and make friends with some of the community's movers and shakers. The effort seemed incredibly relevant and substantive as we worked with big numbers: thousands of voters and millions of dollars. When the election results came one evening in early May, we celebrated a 63-to-37-percent triumph.

Although the overwhelming victory was sweet, it was also anti-climactic. It meant the end of an enjoyable and personally rewarding experience. This type of community involvement woke up something inside my professional spirit and changed my career forever. To make up for the post-election void in my life, I quickly volunteered for the reelection campaign of our local congressman, which also turned out to be a victorious effort.

In the years since then, I have participated in numerous political campaigns, and on a couple occasions, I even served as a campaign manager or a treasurer. About half the campaigns ended in victory. Others were terribly disappointing, but even in defeat, the effort was worthwhile. For a volunteer like me, the value was in the process. The personal benefits came from simply being involved.

My schedule is now more demanding, leaving me little time for political campaigning, but I am grateful I've done so much of it. Political campaigning got me noticed. It started me down a track to much greater success in all aspects of my career. Watching politicians ply their trade taught me a great deal about getting noticed in the business world.

Successful people in any professional field must behave like politicians. Now, I'm not saying we adopt the stereotypically seedy and nefarious character traits that too many politicians exhibit. Rather, we must accept the fact that every one of us is in a lifelong, personal "campaign."

In order to get ahead and reach our dreams, we must promote ourselves at every opportunity. For our entire lives, we are trying perpetually to get "elected" to something. While it may not be an election per se, we're all trying to win "votes" in our own, individual ways. Perhaps you are trying to land a new job or get a promotion. Maybe you are trying to attract a new client. Maybe you covet a position on a prestigious committee. No matter what you hope to do or accomplish, you are well advised to behave like a politician.

Politicians understand better than anyone else that they are selling themselves. Nothing matters more to a politician than name recognition and a positive reputation. Politicians know that most voters rely on name recognition and familiarity when deciding which way to cast their votes. It goes something like this: Voters go to the polls and look over the ballot. While voters may know about the presidential and congressional candidates, chances are they have not studied the lesser races. They see the names of two candidates and one jumps out. "I've heard of him," the voter thinks and chooses the one who seems familiar.

You are a brand. *You* are a business of one.

Good politicians know that their names are like brands. Just as Procter & Gamble spends millions of dollars promoting each of its products, a politician invests money in his or her name and reputation. Just as a *Fortune 500* company has a strategic plan to promote itself, a politician carefully maps out a strategy that makes the politician known to the electorate. A politician works hard to craft a deliberately planned image. That image is analogous to a brand.

This personal branding behavior is not unique to politics. It replicates itself in the business world and in all professional arenas. Make no mistake about it: You need to establish a well-known name and reputation if you hope to get ahead. Like a politician, you must build yourself up in the public eye. You must create a "personal brand."

You are a brand. *You* are a business of one.

Regardless of your age or chosen career field, you have a personal brand, a reputation that must be carefully maintained and vigorously promoted. No matter how modest you are, sometimes you have to toot your own horn.

Professionals must promote their personal brands to be noticed in a competitive world. Whether you're hoping for a promotion, striving to bag your biggest client ever, or just trying to make a difference in your community, one thing is for sure: You have to stand out. There is no room for shrinking violets in today's world; successful people are bold.

As you are surely aware, we now work in a global economy in which people, jobs and capital move freely all over the world. In a split second, your job can be eliminated and your life turned upside down. If you're a good self marketer, you have much less to fear. Someone who has built a well-known name, a great reputation and a lot of community goodwill can bounce back quickly and grab another, perhaps better opportunity.

In a world full of downsizing, rightsizing, outsourcing and offshoring, today's employees are essentially free agents. Even if you're classified as a traditional employee, it's time to start thinking like an independent contractor. You are no longer beholden to one company, to one employer. You have options. If you think about it, that's quite liberating. You can do whatever you want. People have career choices today that were unfathomable a generation ago.

The English philosopher John Locke once said, "Every man has a property in his own person. This nobody has a right to, but himself." These words had a direct philosophical effect on the founding of the United States in the 18th century, but they have never been truer than they are now. In 21st century America, we enjoy historically unprecedented freedoms.

Although you own your personal brand and all the privileges pertaining thereto, it comes with a burden. You bear the responsibility for building that brand, shaping it and promoting it to the general public. As a good self marketer, you can recruit the services of others, but the responsibility to carry out a good marketing strategy is solely yours. No one is going to go out of the way to seek out your potential. You must develop it and proclaim it to the masses.

Building a bigger and better image is not easy, but anyone with at least a moderate level of talent and intelligence can do it. Motivation is the key. As the great motivational author, Norman Vincent Peale, said, there is tremendous power in positive thinking. Now is the time for optimism. Tell yourself you can create the personal brand you really want. Be committed to it and don't let other people or any haunting feelings of self doubt stand in your way. Like the politician running for office, you have to stick your neck out and take a little risk when you promote yourself in public. Not only is it worth the risk, but establishing a well-known and respected brand is essential in our modern culture. A good reputation is such an important professional asset that they ought to have a line reserved for it on personal financial statements!

The world is more competitive than ever. Today's marketplace is noisier than ever. It's hard to stand out and establish a good reputation. Successful people must know how to promote their brands in this big, loud and sometimes intimidating world. That's what this book is all about. In the coming chapters, we will explore the secrets of marketing yourself. I'll give you proven techniques designed to get you noticed and earn you the respect of others.

It's time to start a new chapter in your lifelong campaign for excellence. It's time to build up your name and get noticed. It will take a lot of hard work and perhaps a new way of thinking, but you can do it.

Are you ready to change your future?

CHAPTER ONE

What is Self Marketing?

MOST OF THE WORLD'S GREAT RELIGIONS ENCOURAGE US TO LIVE A humble life. Humility is a virtue. We are taught to put the interests of others before our own and to practice modesty. In the Christian faith, pride is considered one of the seven deadly sins. We are taught since early childhood to show some respectful modesty in the company of others.

Back in 1937, Dale Carnegie wrote one of the most useful books in the history of Western civilization, *How to Win Friends and Influence People*. In this groundbreaking work, Carnegie argued that interpersonal skills were far more important than financial skills or any other set of skills in determining one's success. Specifically, Carnegie preached humility. Essentially, he said you can get another person to like you if you avoid using the word "*I*" and focus on using the other person's first name, which he said was "the sweetest word in the English language." Carnegie went further, telling us that we should talk about the other person's interests instead of our own. Carnegie's beliefs must hold some merit, because his book continues to sell millions of copies and even spawned a business designed to help people succeed.

President Abraham Lincoln, perhaps the greatest leader America has ever known, mastered Carnegie's principles decades before Carnegie was born. Lincoln achieved phenomenal success in a time of unimaginable hardship by being kind to others, talking about others' interests, giving credit to others (especially his subordinates) and by suggesting rather than demanding. Lincoln is historical proof that you can be amazingly successful by living a life of modesty and humility.

Millions of people have read Carnegie's book, generations of Americans have been influenced by Abraham Lincoln's leadership principles, and billions of people around the world engage in religious activities. That means a lot of people have learned that humility and modesty are not only virtuous, they can also help you get ahead in life.

> In a book about "self marketing," one of the first things that must be acknowledged is the virtue of humility.

Modesty and humility are so burned into our brains, that most of us have a strong dislike for anyone who comes across as boastful, conceited or overly self interested. Nobody likes braggarts, show-offs, know-it-alls and blowhards. You probably know someone who boasts too much or promotes himself or herself too zealously. In almost every organization, there is at least one person who shamelessly elevates himself or herself often to the detriment of others.

Don't be that person.

In a book about "self marketing," one of the first things that must be acknowledged is the virtue of humility. There is a fine line between good, healthy self promotion and egotistical boasting. Without question, you need to be bold when marketing yourself in a loud and crowded marketplace. The key to self marketing is to promote yourself while making it look as if you're not trying. Let people know what you're doing without being obnoxious.

Self marketing is more art than science. There's a fine line between self marketing and egotistical boasting. While avoiding boastfulness is important, self marketing does require confidence. As President Woodrow Wilson said, "All the extraordinary men I have known were extraordinary in their own estimation." In other words, you must believe in yourself before anyone else will. It is necessary to have some humility, but you can't be great if you don't believe the potential is inside you.

You can promote yourself without appearing to brag as long as the self promotion meets five criteria: It is strategically planned, consistent, exercised skillfully, tasteful and carried out for legitimate, ethical and moral reasons.

Strategically Planned

Just as major corporations have strategic marketing plans, so should you, since you are essentially a business unto yourself. Successful organizations spend copious hours, involving leaders from all departments, to craft strategic marketing plans. While you don't have "departments" within yourself, you do need a good plan for how you will announce your wonderful deeds and attributes to the rest of the world.

Later in this book, I will give you specific advice on how to plan your personal marketing strategy. In chapter 12, we will discuss "How to Think Like a Marketer." In chapter 15, we will discuss how goal setting can help you accomplish your personal strategic marketing plan. But for now, let's just say you need a well–thought-out, written plan to promote yourself.

You will need to assess your strengths and weaknesses. Think about how to minimize attention on your weaknesses while maximizing exposure of your strengths. You also must assess what opportunities and threats are out there that could have an impact on your personal image-building efforts.

It will be necessary to define your target audience – the group of people to whom your self marketing message is directed. It is too expensive and physically daunting to market yourself to all 6 billion people on earth. Identify who you most need to impress and focus your attention on them. If you happen to impress people outside your target audience, that's just frosting on the cake.

Once you have all this figured out, you will need a system or mechanism to deliver your message to the target audience. The actual delivery method of your self marketing plan is where this book devotes much of its focus. You portray your image to your target audience by using the mass media to your advantage. This can mean a lot of different things: You may submit original writings to newspapers and magazines. You may become an expert in a particular subject area and thus make yourself available to reporters as an expert source. You may decide to become a press-release-writing machine, sending out notices of anything newsworthy that you do.

As a freelance writer and a radio talk-show host, I have seen firsthand the powerful self marketing benefits that come from using the media. Thousands of people listen to my radio show and read my newspaper columns. That has led to more business opportunities for me and my company.

In addition to harnessing the media, you may choose to promote your image by networking and getting involved in an array of civic, professional and social organizations. I'm sure you know people who do such a good job of networking that they are seemingly "everywhere." There is no limit to the number of methods you can use to communicate your reputation to your target audience. The key is to plan ahead before you start doing the actual communication.

If your self marketing is strategically planned, it will come across as more sincere and less like egotistical boasting. It will prevent you from wasting time on activities that have a low level of effectiveness.

Consistent

Good self marketing is consistent. People like consistency in other people. Others will be more comfortable around you if they have a good idea how you will behave in a given situation. If you are consistent in your public actions and behavior, the promotion you do will seem natural and less like boasting and bragging.

Consistency relates to one of the most important concepts in marketing: frequency. Whether you are networking with other people, getting quoted in the newspaper or being interviewed on the television news, frequency is critical. As consumers of news and information, people need to hear things over and over again. There's an old saying in advertising that you have to repeat a name seven times in a single radio commercial in order for the listener to remember it. For some reason, we tend not to remember things we hear unless we hear them consistently.

Frequency does not only relate to the number of times we hear a name in a given commercial, we must hear that commercial regularly over the course of time. I could spend millions of dollars for an advertisement during the biggest football telecast of the year. For 60 seconds, I could stand in front of the camera, repeating my name over and over again. Millions of people would see it, and would talk about what a strange commercial it is, but virtually nobody would remember me a few weeks later. In order to establish positive name recognition, you must make an impression with targeted audience members consistently and regularly over the course of time.

In personal marketing, that means you need to be in front of people each week, preferably each day. It means that you go to that business networking event at the end of the day even though you are tired. It means you get up early and meet a prospective client for morning coffee before going to the office. It means you think of creative ways to get your name in the news. Self marketing is a 24-hour-a-day obligation. It is a perpetual responsibility, the lifelong political campaign for your personal election.

Exercised Skillfully

To be effective in self marketing, you need to acquire the right set of skills. For some, these skills seem to come naturally, almost like an innate talent from God. For others, developing good self marketing skills is a painful, arduous journey taken over many years. Regardless of how adept you are now, you can always improve. Skillful execution means that you can market your personal brand without looking like a shameless self promoter.

Throughout this book, I will share what these skills are and how to use them. That's just the start, however. Mastery of the self marketing skills comes only after a great deal of practice. The best way to develop them is to go out into the world and use them. If you fall flat on your face a couple of times, it may be embarrassing, but failure is a great teacher. In order to hone these skills, get out and exercise them.

Tasteful

Tasteful self promotion is closely related to the skillful promotion just defined. People who are not tasteful in their self marketing efforts are boorish. Tasteful self marketers know the appropriate time and place to self promote, but they also know when to shut their mouths. Just as good leaders must know how to follow, a gifted self marketer must know when to embrace silence. Tasteful self marketers are polite, courteous and do not try to dominate conversations. They embrace the rules of social etiquette. They tell people about their impressive accomplishments, but they spend a great deal of time asking questions and showing interest in others. Such people are confident, but they also work hard, letting their actions account for a significant part of their self promotion.

You must be able to accept constructive criticism open mindedly and praise graciously.

A tasteful self marketer is a nice person, who treats all people well. You must be able to accept constructive criticism open mindedly and praise graciously. A tasteful self promoter answers praise with a smile and a "thank-you." He or she does not immediately dispute the criticism, nor diminish the praise.

For Legitimate, Ethical and Moral Reasons

Morality should form the foundation of your self marketing efforts, for if you are doing it for noble reasons, you will be more believable and trustworthy. If your primary motivation is to massage your insatiable ego, people will be able to tell. You must also be careful that your self marketing is never done at the expense of others. If you gossip or denigrate someone else as you work to build up yourself, you will be perceived negatively, as someone with a self-esteem problem.

In order for your target audience to embrace your self marketing efforts, first make sure you are doing it for the right reasons: These could be to advance your career, recruit a new employee, earn more business, further your cause, get elected to an office, land an appointment on a board or prestigious committee or make a difference in your community. These are legitimate reasons to self market.

Ultimately, your self marketing should pass a little test. Answer this question: "If people knew the real reason why I am engaging in this activity, would I be embarrassed?" If the answer is "no," you're okay.

SELF-MARKETING IS PERSONAL BRANDING

Ultimately, you need to keep reminding yourself that you are in a lifelong personal campaign and that you are a brand that needs to be marketed.

Marketing can be defined in a number of ways. To some, it is simply the facilitation of buying and selling. Others describe it as everything involved in moving a product or service from the seller to the buyer. An old definition of marketing refers to the four "P's" that comprise it: product, place, promotion and price. A more in-depth definition would describe it as a process, from planning to execution, which identifies consumers for a specific product, communicates how the product satisfies consumer wants and needs and spurs the consumer to make a purchase. Marketing also relates to the creation, maintenance and expansion of customer groups. Marketers focus on managing relationships with customers.

Promotion is a subset of marketing. It has to do with the communication activities that give consumers product information in an attempt to persuade them to buy. Promotion could include advertising, direct "personal" selling and sales promotions.

A brand is both symbolic and tangible depending on your perspective. It is a trademark, a distinctive name, and a combination of images that creates associations and expectations in the minds of consumers. Brands are symbolic embodiments of a product that publicly distinguish that product from all other competitors. As advertising guru David Ogilvy said, a brand is the "intangible sum of a product's attributes."

These definitions of marketing, promotion and brand assume a *company* is working to sell a product or service to customers. In your life-long self marketing campaign, *you* are the "brand." The work you do and the value you add are the "product." Once you accept this, you are ready to start promoting yourself.

No Room for Shrinking Violets: Why You Must Market Yourself

CONSTRUCTION EXECUTIVE WAS TALKING TO ME RECENTLY ABOUT HOW the job-bidding process has changed in his industry. It used to be that a corporation would announce plans to build a building before hiring a general contractor. The construction companies would then make contact with the owner and try to win the business. That is no longer the case.

Nowadays, as soon we hear the first wisp of a rumor about a new building project, chances are the entire construction team is already in place. The successful construction company is the one that is building relationships and discussing ideas with real estate developers long before anyone puts pencil to paper. To win contracts, construction companies need to be marketing themselves and aggressively going after business even before developers are imagining their projects.

In business, relationships are more important today than at any other time in modern history. That's a bold statement when you consider the impersonality that the Internet has brought to the business world. Nevertheless, because there is such tremendous competition, relationships matter. Successful professionals build relationships immediately with the hope that they will bring business some day. As a self marketer, you must be patient, because you never know when a good relationship will lead to more dollars in your pocket.

Why must we market ourselves? In short, we have no choice.

Long-standing relationships are hard to break, which is why they are so valuable. That's also why we must start building relationships with as many people as possible and be patient until a relationship leads to some opportunity.

As a part-time faculty member, I teach a real estate brokerage course at the University of Nebraska. Much of the semester focuses on sales techniques used by real estate agents. I tell my students that they must actively search for and build new relationships, but that they can not expect every relationship to bear fruit immediately.

One of my former students, a very talented one, passed her real estate licensure exam and affiliated with a large residential brokerage company. She came from a locally prominent family, was active in the community and had a large network of friends. She was dismayed on two separate occasions when a family member and good friend chose NOT to use her as their real estate agent. You see, these people had bought and sold houses before and chose to keep their former real estate agents. Why? The agents had done a great job for them and had built relationships that were too strong for the unproven newbie to break. My former student was persistent. She marketed herself to everyone she knew and to thousands of people she had never met. A year later, she had built plenty of professional relationships and was doing big deals.

Why must we market ourselves? In short, we have no choice. There really is no place left for the "shrinking violet," the quiet, shy person who waits passively for the business to come to him or her. Passive behavior is out, assertive behavior is expected, and sometimes a little aggressive behavior is necessary. We are operating in a highly competitive, fast-paced, global economy that doesn't take time to stop and smell the roses. We must keep up in order to avoid being trampled to death.

There have never been more highly educated people in the history of the world. Colleges and universities are pumping out scads of newly minted graduates who expect to make big salaries and achieve success. Furthermore, the competition no longer comes just from fellow Americans. Countries such as China and India, which together have more than 2 billion people, are modernizing and ramping up their competitiveness at an alarming rate. Even if your job is local in nature, the rise of international competition has at least an indirect effect on you.

It is a simple fact: The world is a bigger, noisier, more competitive, more crowded and faster place. Just to be noticed and respected, sometimes you have to beat your chest, pound your own drum and toot your own horn.

While increased competition is reason enough to market yourself, there are others. As a successful person, you have a number of reasons for building and promoting your own personal brand:

1. For the benefit of your own career,
2. To increase your name recognition,
3. To boost your personal reputation,
4. To promote your employer's business,
5. To get new clients, and
6. To further your ideological, civic or social beliefs or a pet cause.

CAREER BENEFIT

Career advancement is the most obvious reason to promote yourself and the most likely reason you will engage in it. If you want to land a new job or be promoted where you currently work, you must engage in self promotion.

To get a new job with a different employer, a number of good self marketing techniques will be necessary. For one thing, you need to know how to interview properly. This means building rapport with the hiring manager and showing how you can be a benefit to the new organization. This is accomplished by communicating clearly how your skills and experience would match the new job. Good inter- viewees know how to market themselves during the awkward, intimi- dating and artificial process that is a job interview.

More importantly, good self marketing is often necessary to land an interview in the first place. Approximately two-thirds of jobs are never advertised; they are part of the "hidden job market." These jobs go to insiders – people who know the right people or to specifically recruit- ed candidates. Often jobs are specially created for certain professionals who possess just the right talent or experience to help a company.

If these jobs are "hidden," you have to know how and where to "find" them. That comes through self marketing. By putting yourself out in public, getting involved and taking leadership positions in your industry, you develop that personal brand I've been talking about. If you build that brand properly, it will eventually be very appealing to some employer. In fact, your brand could be so appealing that an employer may pull out all the stops just to get you on board.

I know several people who enjoy custom-made jobs just because their future employers knew about them through networking and other self marketing activities. I'm actually one of those people. My last two jobs were created for me.

In some industries, where there are acute shortages of talent, you can sit in your office, isolated from the world and somehow the headhunters (professional recruiters) will still find you. In most professions, that's not the case. You cannot afford to be passive. You need to be out there build- ing a reputation, a brand. Just like the politician campaigning for office, you need to build name recognition, because you are always campaign- ing for the next step in your career – a bigger and better job.

Even when you are still new in a job you absolutely love, you need to get out into the community or industry and market the hell out of yourself. You never know how long it will take and how much self marketing effort it will take to land the next big job, so you should start early. Furthermore, you never know when you could be suddenly terminated from a job. The more people you know and the more people who have been exposed to your personal brand, the faster you can bounce back with another, perhaps better, job.

NAME RECOGNITION

As we will discuss in much greater detail in chapter four, self marketing success begins with name recognition. The political hopeful running for office knows that nothing will help win the election more than strong name recognition. It is just as important in other professional arenas.

For some reason, people are more impressed with you if they've heard of you. If someone believes an unusually large number of other people know you, they see you as bigger, more successful and more powerful, and thus more desirable to be around. Perception is reality. Even if you are no more talented than the next person, you can get ahead of that person by having name recognition. Think of all the Hollywood celebrities who use their fame to influence people with their political and social philosophies. In real life, a lot of actors and rock stars are lightly educated posers, yet too many people assume they are experts worth following, simply because of their fame.

Developing a high level of name recognition is simply one of the single most important things you can do to further your career. I'm not saying you need to develop a name as widely recognized as a movie star's, a senator's or a best-selling author's, but within your field of expertise, you need to become a mini rock star. If you're in business, you should strive to be a local celebrity. Name recognition is power. Why do you think so many star athletes become insurance salespeople and financial advisers after they retire from sports? It's because people revere them. The well-known professional can parlay his or her public adoration into real dollars.

PERSONAL REPUTATION

A better reputation is a good reason to market yourself. We all like to associate with people who are esteemed and respected. As I've said before, a good reputation is one of your most important professional assets, and it needs to be protected at all times.

Tactfully, you need to make people aware of your good deeds and behavior. You can develop a positive reputation with a small number of people simply by exhibiting the right behavior on a consistent basis. Building a strong reputation with a larger group of people takes some carefully planned self marketing. You simply don't have time to develop a personal relationship with everyone you might need to impress. That's where self marketing comes in. First, you build a trusted core group of people who love you and believe in you. From there, you use the self marketing principles in this book to project the image you want everyone else to see.

PROMOTING YOUR COMPANY

Regardless of what job roles we have, we are all essentially working in sales.

If you are employed by a company or an organization, you have a moral obligation to promote your employer. Every employee should do his or her part to further the organization. Regardless of what job roles we have, we are all essentially working in sales.

Much of this book's content is frankly self-centered; it is "you-centric." The book's purpose is to help you get ahead as an individual. With that said, you ought to use your self marketing powers for the good of your company. You should use your personal brand to help promote your company.

Fortunately, this is not merely an exercise in altruism on your part; it's a win-win situation. By using your personal brand, reputation and recognized name to help your company, you fulfill your ethical obligations and help the company make more money. The better the company does, the more likely you are to stay employed and get raises or bonuses. Anything you do to market your employer in turn promotes you. You can then use your company as a way to become a mini rock star in your profession.

ACQUIRE NEW CLIENTS

My alarm clock goes off at 6:00 a.m. every Saturday. When most people are enjoying sleeping in on the weekend, I'm getting up to prepare for *Grow Omaha*, the weekly radio talk show I host with Trenton Magid. *Grow Omaha* focuses on economic development in the Omaha, Nebraska, metropolitan area. My co-host and I work at Coldwell Banker Commercial World Group, a commercial real estate company. As people who sell and lease property, manage buildings and develop real estate, our work is closely related to economic development. We love economic development, and we love the community in which we live, so it is natural for us to produce such a show.

While affection for our city is one reason why we give up our Saturday mornings, another big reason is to promote our company and acquire new clients.

Since starting this radio show, we have added correlated marketing activities. I write a bi-weekly newspaper column on economic development for *The City Weekly,* and I give speeches to community and professional groups. All of these activities have led directly to the acquisition of new clients. By engaging in highly public work, we have established a good name and legitimacy in our community. When someone opens the phone book looking for a commercial real estate company, we sound familiar. We're credible. We're a safe choice.

Fortunately, you don't have to start your own radio show to get more clients. You simply need to make yourself known; you need to promote your personal brand. This can be done by calling people, asking someone to meet you for coffee and showing up at business networking events. My colleague likes to tell people that he once landed a real estate listing after striking up a conversation with someone in a supermarket check-out line. This may sound a little weird, but I know of one real estate agent who ended up doing a deal by starting a conversation with some dude in the locker room shower at the gym!

You never know where the opportunity will come to land a new client. That's why you must market yourself constantly to everyone you meet.

BELIEFS AND CAUSES

Last but not least, you should market yourself to build influence in civic, philanthropic and political affairs. I'm sure you have certain beliefs that you hold near and dear to your heart. You may have a pet cause, something that juices your emotions and pushes you to act. Perhaps you want to become a community activist working to improve safety in your neighborhood. You might have a passion for animals and want to support your local humane shelter. Maybe you are sick of the high taxes you pay, so you decide to join an anti-tax lobbying organization.

Regardless of who you are, there is probably something that fires you up. By building a big name, a strong personal brand and a great reputation, you simply have more power to effect change. There's nothing more fun than throwing your weight around in advocacy of something that stirs your passions.

CHAPTER THREE

The 8 Critical Rules of the Game and How to Win

MARKETING YOURSELF IS KIND OF LIKE A GAME. AT LEAST, YOU ARE MORE likely to be successful at it if you think of it as a game and decide to have some fun while doing it. Like every game, self marketing has some basic rules.

RULE #1: POSITIVE THINKING

Nothing is more important in the self marketing game than a positive, can-do attitude. You must go into your self marketing endeavors believing your efforts will be fruitful. You must believe that you are a strong, talented, successful person who has something worth marketing. While not every little thing you do to market yourself will bring you instant opportunities, it is important to realize that many things in totality will eventually bring great success.

As I do things to promote my personal reputation or my company, I remind myself that every activity helps. Even if I have only one meaningful conversation at a networking event, I know meeting that one new person could lead to an opportunity.

Your mental outlook is at least half of what it takes to be successful. Positive thinking will help you be persistent – a key component of success in the professional world. Most of the great corporate executives and political leaders throughout history have been insufferably optimistic. Optimism motivates them to keep pushing and pushing. By constantly believing that their visions will come to fruition, they keep their people focused on the end goal. In your personal business of one, you need to set goals, work diligently and never stop believing that you will accomplish them.

RULE #2: DEVELOP AN EXPERTISE

It is much easier to promote yourself if you are an expert in something. Perhaps to your surprise, becoming an expert in something is not necessarily difficult. You don't have to have an academic degree in your area of expertise (although that certainly helps). Experts are "opinion leaders," the types of people from whom other people take cues and get ideas.

An expertise gives you something upon which to focus your marketing efforts. It gives you legitimacy. Once you are an expert, you go from being an ordinary person to someone whom people want to listen to. You become fascinating, enlightening and engaging, even though on the inside, you still feel like your same old self.

So how do you become an expert? First, I recommend that you literally sit down in a quiet room with a piece of paper. Write down every subject you can think of that interests you and that you think you could possibly learn enough about to someday become an expert. At this point, don't worry too much about practicality – if it pops into your head, write it down. It is okay to dream about the areas of expertise you would like to master. In fact, I encourage you to dream big.

Don't stifle yourself. If even a tiny part of you wants to master a certain area of expertise, write it down.

Study your list carefully and think of the areas of expertise that would most interest you. Next, think of the ones that would be most realistic, most closely related to your career and most marketable to a target audience.

Once you have identified the area of expertise that is best for you, it is then time to immerse yourself in it. You must study it inside and out, forward and back. Read journals. Go to seminars and conferences. Search for it on the Internet and study every relevant website you can. Find other people who are interested in the same subject area and make contact with them. You will be able to share ideas with them and use their knowledge to further your expertise.

Several years ago, I decided upon an area of expertise to pursue. I wanted something that blended my talents and interests with my profession: commercial real estate. I gave this a great deal of thought.

First of all, I've always been fairly adept at communication. I studied journalism in college and had done a great deal of marketing and public relations work in my career. Second, I have always been fascinated with cities – the way they develop, the way they foster entrepreneurialism and how they create wealth. Third, with a master's degree in political science and public administration, I have always been fascinated with the policy-making process. I enjoyed studying how polarized interest groups competed in the public arena of ideas. Fourth, I have always been a proud booster of Omaha, the city in which I lived and worked. I threw all of these interests into my mental caldron and found inspiration. It came to me one day that I should become an expert in economic development in Omaha. After all, commercial real estate is closely aligned with economic development. It was a natural marriage of my interests and my profession.

With my mind focused on an area of expertise, I set out to develop it. I studied every book and article I could get my hands on that had to do with real estate development, construction, urban planning and business expansion. I read up on census demographics and studied maps. I read everything I could about Omaha's development history. I talked about this stuff at parties and over lunch with friends. I found Internet sites frequented by people who shared my interests. I worked with my boss and colleagues to focus our company on the community's growth and development. Our firm became a real estate company that was also committed to promoting the city and its economy.

This led to a number of good marketing ideas. Soon, I started writing articles in the *Midlands Business Journal,* a weekly business newspaper. Eventually, that led to my regular opinion column, "T-Squares & I-Beams," in *The City Weekly*, which focused on Omaha's growth and development.

The more I learned about economic development, the more people would seek me out. I was once asked to give a speech to a local group about all the real estate development happening in Omaha. The speech went quite well, and someone from the audience asked me to speak to another group. Next thing I knew, I was speaking on the city's growth and development regularly. I now give about 50 of these speeches per year. That led to an even bigger opportunity for me to parlay my new expertise into a great self marketing activity: a radio show.

A good friend of mine, Jim Vokal, was guest-hosting a local radio talk show. The regular host was on vacation and asked Jim to substitute, since Jim was a member of the city council and knew a great deal about local affairs. I was talking with Jim about what he planned to do as substitute host, and he said to me, "You should come on and talk about all the real estate development happening around town."

At first, I thought it was a silly idea. After all, I was just some young guy in commercial real estate. Was I the best source? Weren't there people in the community who were older and wiser than I? Jeez, I had only been in the commercial real estate industry for a couple of years. The thought of going on the radio as a so-called expert before thousands of listeners was intimidating. Nevertheless, I ended up doing it. It turned out great. I received an incredible amount of positive feedback from people who heard the show and thought it was such an interesting topic.

A few weeks later, my boss and good friend Trenton Magid and I were working late and took a dinner break. I told him I had been day-dreaming about talk radio. I imagined the two of us hosting a regular radio show that focused on economic development in Omaha. Practically everything on talk radio was politics, self-help or personal financial planning. I thought it was time for a unique show that discussed interesting aspects of a growing city. Trenton liked the idea and suggested we buy an hour of air time each week and start a show. The *Grow Omaha* radio program went on the air in January 2004.

After a couple years, our show was recruited to KFAB, a 50,000-watt AM station with a primary coverage area extending into several states. Literally thousands of people listen each week. We have a strong base of listeners and many loyal fans. *Grow Omaha* has put Trenton and me into the public eye and has put our company, Coldwell Banker Commercial World Group, even more prominently "on the map." This leads to credibility in the community, making it easier to generate business for our company.

From newspaper articles, to speeches, to the radio program, my involvement with economic development in Omaha is a textbook example of how becoming an expert in something can directly lead to great notoriety and untold opportunities. All you have to do is find your "something."

RULE #3: BE PREPARED

The Boy Scouts have a great motto, which should be adopted by any-one interested in promoting themselves in a noisy, competitive market-place: "be prepared." The Spanish author Miguel de Cervantes said, "To be prepared is half the battle." You never know when an opportunity to promote yourself will arise, so you must always be ready.

Not only must you always be positioned to embrace opportunity, you must also be prepared to deal with challenge.

On September 11, 2001, New York Mayor Rudy Giuliani dealt with a challenge that no other municipal leader in U.S. history had ever faced. The savage terrorism at the World Trade Center that day stunned the world, but it did not destroy the spirit of New York City. A good amount of credit for New York's steadfastness goes to its leader. In his book, *Leadership*, Giuliani said he was able to stay calm in the face of crisis because of preparation, which he defines as "not assuming a damn thing." Giuliani goes further and advocates "relentless preparation," which allows you to anticipate potential trouble before it arrives.

Hopefully, none of us will ever have to lead a city through a 9/11-like disaster, but in our own careers, we must always be prepared. We must have contingencies in place in case the unexpected happens. In self marketing, relentless preparation means you plan what you will say in certain situations. You put a great deal of thought into the things you write and say. It means you have promotional materials for yourself and your company ready to go at a moment's notice. It means that you are mentally prepared for any sort of opportunity or threat that could come flying out of left field at the most unexpected time.

RULE #4: THE RIGHT ATTITUDE

You can't market yourself if you have nothing to market. That means you must work hard at all times. Marketing without solid performance behind it is but a lie. As you promote yourself, you must constantly work hard. The harder you work and the more you produce, the more confident you will feel, and therefore your self marketing efforts will convey better. This creates a snowball effect, because the better your self marketing is, the more opportunities you will have to be productive. A self marketer with a good work ethic will search for opportunities everywhere. Be curious. Sometimes the best ones come from the places you least expect. Constantly be on the lookout for opportunities to promote yourself. Pounce when the opportunities show up.

To be effective in self promotion you must think big and take risks. Sometimes you have to step out of your comfort zone. Perhaps you are somewhat shy or are new to your business and thus intimidated by industry veterans. Don't waste time on fear and worry. It leads to disappointment and inaction. For many people, their first forays into self marketing are small. That's a fine way to gain experience and build self confidence. Grassroots self marketing can start very humbly. The key is to keep building up your efforts. You will never gain the highest levels of name recognition and respect if you don't do something big at some point. Once you break through the big risk "barrier," all subsequent activities will not seem like such a big deal. There is an old saying that life comes down to just a few big moments. Don't let timidity prevent you from seizing big opportunities in your life.

Self marketing is a positive-sum game, not a zero-sum game. Everyone can win. Just because one person becomes a rock star in an industry or community doesn't mean that someone else cannot. Some people, even some successful ones, have a difficult time understanding this. No doubt you have come across someone who can't stand hearing praise about someone else. You say something nice about someone else, and that person feels compelled to refute it, bring up a negative thing about the person or at least minimize it with a quick barb or roll of the eyes. Anyone who behaves like this is telling the rest of the world that he or she has a low self esteem or a compromised sense of self worth.

One of the most important rules of the self marketing game is to never tear down others while promoting yourself. In fact, we should take this rule so seriously that we should go out of our way to build others up as we promote ourselves. Nothing looks so bad as to come across as jealous, envious or spiteful.

RULE #5: EVERYONE COUNTS

To get ahead in business, you need to impress the right people, but you have to be careful. There is a temptation to focus only on those whom you perceive to be powerful. The Scottish philosopher Thomas Carlyle told us in the 19th century: "A great man shows his greatness by the way he treats little men." The seemingly non-powerful people could be powerful indeed. If they lack outright power, they may have influence over those who do have it. Secretaries come to mind. Oftentimes a job candidate will be so focused on impressing the prospective boss that he or she brushes past the secretary without acknowledgment. This could turn out to be a big mistake.

As any professional knows, bosses can be incredibly dependent on a secretary. If the secretary hates a candidate, the boss will probably choose someone else rather than alienate someone upon whom he or she depends. As an outsider, you don't know the hidden relationships that may exist between the powerful person you want to impress and the staff members around the boss. That secretary could be the boss's kid, best friend or even a romantic interest. Treat secretaries and other staff members like gold. Your success may depend on it.

It is wise to think on a long-term basis and market yourself to anyone at any time. You never know who could be your boss someday. You never know who could be a great client someday. Build relationships now to sow the seeds of future opportunity. It is never too early to start networking with people. Any relationship can lead to great opportunity.

I have known my current boss since I was in seventh grade. We had been close friends all through high school, college and our early adult years. In early 2001, I became restless in my position as dean of student services at a private college. I sought the counsel of my friend as I prepared to search for a new career. At the time, his commercial real estate firm was going through a rapid growth cycle and had just affiliated with Coldwell Banker Commercial, an international real estate franchisor. His career advice was to work for him! While at first I had some trepidation about working for such a close friend, it turned out to be a win-win situation for both of us. I moved into an exciting, professionally fulfilling job with a great organization, and he got an experienced administrator who could assist him in running the company.

Clients can come from anywhere, and relationships you currently take for granted could become very valuable. While I was in graduate school, I had a job training and supervising student orientation leaders – the juniors and seniors who gave campus tours to new freshmen.

One of my orientation leaders was Scott Kennedy, an engineering major from a small town in northeast Nebraska. Like all the orientation leaders, Scott was a good-natured, talented kid with a strong academic profile and some solid campus leadership experience. After my graduate assistantship was completed, I moved away from campus and lost touch with the orientation leaders. Several years went by, and I ran into Scott at a local networking function. Turns out, he became a construction executive and had become successful at quite a young age. He and his wife decided to start a side business, and I had the opportunity to represent him in a major land purchase. Since that deal, Scott has referred other business to me. Back when he was an undergraduate learning to give campus tours while walking backwards, I had no idea he would someday be a valuable client, not to mention a good friend.

Furthermore, you never know just who will become a big success in the future and have tremendous decision-making power. Craig Wolf is a guy I have known since the first grade. Growing up, we were typical suburban kids. After a successful tenure in the U.S. Air Force, Craig went to work for C&A Industries, a staffing and human resources company. As an experiment, his boss allowed him to start a medically related division of the firm. It turned out to be a smashing success. In the years since then, Craig has grown that division into a business behemoth, with clients spread across the nation.

The point of these stories is that self marketing should be directed at everyone, including the people who are already close to you. Too many times, we are tempted to focus solely on the people who are far away from us, so hard to reach they are virtually untouchable. In so doing, it is easy to forget that the people already in our spheres of influence are worthy of a great deal of our attention.

RULE #6: YOU ARE BEING WATCHED

During rehearsals, directors often remind their actors to "stay in character." One of the cardinal sins of theater occurs when an actor loses his concentration and allows a glimpse of his real self to pierce his character's façade. Once that happens, it breaks the audience's sense of suspended disbelief, and the actor loses legitimacy. Skillful actors are constantly aware of good stagecraft mechanics. For instance, an actress backstage waiting for her cue to come on stage should never stand close enough to the leg (side) curtains that audience members could see part of her body. A good actor would never leave his microphone on after he exits the stage. Simply put, actors understand they must maintain professionalism and protect the integrity of their character at all costs.

Professionals of any field would be wise to adopt tenets of the dramatic arts. As a professional trying to market yourself, you must always stay in your professional "character." If you make an ass out of yourself in front of someone, you will have a difficult time ever regaining legitimacy in that person's eyes. Furthermore, it's good to use a little showmanship in the business world. By no means does my reference to acting and showmanship mean that you should be lying and deceitful. It does mean you must polish your image and be conscious of how the little details look to your audience.

As a radio talk-show host, I have to incorporate showmanship into my work. For example, there is an old saying that radio people should always assume every microphone is "live" even when you know it is turned off. Being extra careful prevents you from uttering a four-letter word or speaking some nasty gossip and having it accidentally hit the airwaves. In radio, it's just safe to assume that everyone is listening to everything you say at every moment of the day.

In your career, it is likewise safe to assume that you are always being watched or listened to. If you are out with friends on a Friday night, remember that you still have a professional image to maintain. Anytime you are in public, there's a chance that someone you should impress is observing you unknowingly from afar.

The things you do when you assume no one is watching can hurt your career. I remember an interesting incident that occurred back when I was a college dean. One of the positions that reported directly to me was vacant. We received a lot of resumés, but one of them stood head and shoulders above the rest. This candidate was great on paper, and he was equally impressive when I interviewed him over the telephone. I was already assuming that this guy would become my future staff member. We set up an in-person interview for the next day.

Shortly before the scheduled interview, I was sitting in my office, which overlooked the parking lot. A car pulled into one of the visitor stalls below my window. Thinking it might be my candidate, I watched him get out of the car. He looked to be the age I assumed my candidate to be, so I figured it was him. Then something weird happened.

He reached into the back seat of his car and pulled out a neck tie. He then proceeded to use the reflection of himself in the car window to tie his tie. After securing his tie, he reached back into the back car seat and pulled out an electric razor. Using the same window as a mirror, he proceeded to shave right there in our parking lot. After removing his facial hair, he tossed the razor in the car, pulled on his sport coat, grabbed the obligatory leather portfolio that everyone brings to an interview and walked toward the building.

> The things you do when you assume no one is watching can hurt your career.

Two minutes later my phone buzzed. My assistant's voice said, "Jeff, your appointment is here." Sure enough, it was that guy. Interestingly, he did a fantastic job in the interview, but there was no way I would hire him. Anyone who was so clueless about professionalism and image making was not suited for a managerial position at a reputable college. The moral of the story: Always assume you are being watched and evaluated.

RULE #7: EMBRACE PROFESSIONALISM

Your behavior and image are critical parts of self marketing.

One of the most important things you can do to get ahead is to be nice. Unfortunately, too many business people are the opposite of nice. They think that business success comes from being shrewd, aggressive and selfish. Perhaps they watch too much television or too many mafia movies, but these people believe they must never show kindness, warmth or even the slightest hint of emotional vulnerability. Such people are obsessed with not only winning but thoroughly vanquishing anyone whom they consider a rival. If you practice this type of behavior at work, flush it and get a new outlook.

To succeed, you must be assertive, but aggressive behavior will have a long-term negative effect on your career. A truly professional person is nice, sincerely nice, consistently nice. By being friendly and likeable, you will actually be more successful in a competitive environment. Many of the business negotiations in which we engage are inherently adversarial. That's a fact of life, but it doesn't give you license to be a jerk. Civility is not just a moral-social norm; adopting it is in your best interest. Nice people eventually finish first.

In addition to treating people well, professionalism implies a certain image. If you want to market yourself, make sure you have the right look. You never know when you will run into a member of your personal target audience, so make sure you always look presentable.

Professionals should always be sharply dressed. Some people with big jobs act professionally during the business day. Then you run into them at the supermarket, and they look like hell warmed over. Even when you are "off duty," you are still being watched; the higher you go, the more people will be constantly judging you. That means you can't afford to be seen at the mall looking like a bag lady. Clothing should be neat, clean and appropriately pressed. Shoes, bags and accessories should be in good shape. Personal hygiene is critical. A professional image means you always have a supply of your business cards with you and a pen to write notes. Your car should be uncluttered on the inside and clean on the outside. It would be silly to spend all sorts of time and money promoting yourself when your basic appearance is flawed.

RULE #8: COMMUNICATE CLEARLY

Before stepping into the public arena, think about what you have to say and how you will say it. An effective self marketer knows that communication is critical. Your peers will judge you in large part based upon the quality of your communication. Study your area of expertise and be prepared to field questions about it. Have answers ready, so you don't fumble like an idiot, struggling with an unexpected question.

Your communication with other professionals needs to be interesting, engaging and at times, curiosity-peaking. Just as important is the need to be clear and concise. To be concise, I recommend you develop a personal 30-second "elevator speech." That means you can give a person a basic understanding of who you are and what you do in half a minute, or about the time it takes to ride an elevator in a typical office building.

When devising your elevator speech, be committed to clarity. I go to a lot of networking events. Inevitably, I'll meet someone who can't explain who or what they are. I'll ask such a person, "What do you do?" I might get an answer like this: "I facilitate broad-spectrum, strategic and integrated solutions for financial-service providers, who are re-engineering their organizational paradigms." What on earth does that mean? Sadly, there are way too many people who utter such gibberish at cocktail parties. Instead of sounding important and impressive, they're just annoying. If you want to impress people with what you do, explain it enthusiastically, confidently and in clear-spoken English.

A better elevator speech might sound like this:

"So many companies struggle with strategic planning, especially financial services companies. What I do is sit down with business owners, and for a flat fee, I examine everything they're doing right and wrong. I then create a strategic plan in a format that's easy to share with employees and investors. If they're interested, I'll also hold a workshop for the entire staff. I've been doing this for 10 years and have clients nationwide."

This elevator speech gets to the point and places an image in the listener's mind. As you craft your elevator speech, be brief, descriptive and paint an interesting picture.

MOVING FORWARD

We have now established what self marketing is and why you must engage in it. We've laid the ground rules you must follow. Now it's time to roll up our sleeves and get to work. The next several chapters will give you practical ways you can actually get your message out, promote your personal brand and build your reputation.

Who Are You?
It All Starts With
Name Recognition

I ONCE VOLUNTEERED ON THE POLITICAL CAMPAIGN OF A LOCAL BUSINESS-
man who was running for city council. During the campaign, I
attended a number of political events, but one candidates' forum
stood out in my mind. Candidates from each city council district gathered in a high school gym in front of an audience comprised of community activists, neighborhood leaders, local busy-bodies and a
smattering of other interested persons. Each candidate had just a couple minutes to tout his or her candidacy.

An odd-looking fellow – a long-shot, political newcomer who ended
up losing in a landslide – had the most unique speech. He stood at the
podium and said, "They tell me that political campaigning is all about
name recognition. If that's the case, my name is…" He proceeded to
repeat his name over and over again in a melodic/rhythmic way. He
would say a couple sentences of substance and then once again repeat
his name over and over. It was cute. People laughed. I'm not sure how
seriously the audience took him, but he made an impression. I vividly
remember that stump speech many years later.

While this nontraditional politician didn't win (he had no money for commercials or yard signs), he was right about one thing – it's all about name recognition. At the very basic level, a politician running for office must focus first and foremost on establishing name recognition. The same thing applies to any professional working in any field. If you are going to market yourself, you must establish a recognized name among members of your personal target audience.

LEARNING FROM THE POLITICOS

Political campaign strategy can teach us a great deal about our own self marketing. In establishing name recognition, politicians are good role models. We must think like politicians, because each of us is in a lifelong personal campaign.

Politicians build campaign strategies that are fundamentally based upon establishing a name. Frankly, the average voter is politically unsophisticated and poorly informed about election issues and candidates. Although I have a master's degree in political science, I must confess that this often applies to me too. Sure, I'll be quite knowledgeable about some candidates or ballot issues, but there are always a few about whom I know nothing. When the typical voter comes to an obscure part of the ballot, where candidates for something like the Mosquito Abatement District are listed, chances are the voter knows very little. In this situation, the typical voter first looks at the names to see if he or she recognizes any of them. If one name sounds more familiar than the others, that is who gets an "X" in the box.

> We must think like politicians, because each of us is in a lifelong personal campaign.

Politicians know this, and they act accordingly. That's why most political advertising is so image oriented and not focused on complicated policy issues. That's why you see acres and acres of yard signs littering the cityscape during each election cycle. It's why we are inundated on radio and television with fatiguing political commercials.

Pay close attention, and you'll notice that each commercial says or shows the candidate's name multiple times in a 30- or 60-second timeframe.

Campaign consultants know that their political clients must use a variety of media, a "media mix," to develop name recognition. In order to plant your name firmly in each voter's cranium, you must penetrate their personal lives. To do this, politicians come at us through television, radio, U.S. mail, and in most local races they literally knock on our doors. They know that frequency matters, which is why the same signs pop up everywhere and the same commercials air over and over again.

A politician doesn't miss a parade, pancake feed, major sporting event or any Catholic fish fry on a Lenten Friday. Any gathering of potential voters becomes a politician magnet. Campaign managers work feverishly to get their candidates on the news, hopefully portrayed in a positive light. Everything is focused on getting as many positive impressions as possible without the candidate saying anything of deep substance.

There's no question: In politics, business and personal marketing, it all begins with name recognition. Like politicians, businesses repeat their names or brand names over and over again, using a carefully chosen media mix. It works. When customers flip through the Yellow Pages, looking under "Real Estate," they will find a list of several real estate companies. On paper, they all look the same. Who will they call? Most likely, they will choose a company they've heard of. To most customers, a familiar name feels like a safe choice.

In politics, voters rely on the candidate's name identification. In business, customers rely on familiarity. Because YOU are a business unto yourself, and because you are engaged in a lifelong campaign to promote yourself, you must establish strong name recognition and personal brand awareness right now.

CULT OF CELEBRITY

Gaining familiarity and becoming a "safe choice" is not the only reason why you must build name recognition. You need to become somewhat of a celebrity, even if it's in your own little way. It's unlikely that

- 33 -

you would ever become famous like a movie star, nor would most people want to be, but you can become famous inside your sphere of interest. Your fame can exist solely in a certain industry, your community
or among those who share your interests. Fame
can be widespread or narrowly focused.
However you decide to define it, you need to
become a rock star in something.

For better or worse, our society is obsessed with celebrity.

For better or worse, our society is obsessed
with celebrity. We love to be around famous
people. For whatever reason, we assume that
someone who is known by a lot of other people
is someone to whom we should cater. We
assume that fame is synonymous with power,
wealth and inside access. Because other people –
especially well-known people – often look better
on the outside than they actually feel on the inside, we tend to perceive
them as something more than they really are. When we get bored with
our own everyday lives, it is easy to become infatuated with a famous
person who appears to have so much excitement in his or her life.

Otherwise balanced and rational people have been known to get wob-
bly kneed in the presence of celebrities. I once encountered one of the
world's best-known actresses outside the Ritz-Carlton Hotel in Chicago.
It was interesting watching people swarm around her like hyenas scav-
enging a dead animal. I was disgusted with it, but then as we were walking away, I kept turning my head back to look at her. She was glamorous
and attractive, much prettier in person than on the big screen. I wanted
to see what she was doing, how she was handling the circus around her.
Suddenly, I realized I was staring. I was no different than the jackals
around her. I was intrigued by her celebrity, and I was frustrated with
myself for my simple-minded behavior – following the herd.

Celebrity is such a powerful force that it warps our perception. An
unknown comedian can give one of the best comedy routines you've
ever heard – the audience will enjoy it and appreciate it, but the
comedian will receive only the standard round of applause at the end.
A world-famous comedian can do a mediocre job and get an uproar-

ious ovation. The audience simply *wants* the famous comedian to be the funniest.

I once attended a convention in Orlando where the keynote speaker was a famous basketball coach. He was one of the best-known coaches in the National Basketball Association with one of the highest winning percentages. He gave an utterly mediocre speech. Nevertheless, grown men were drooling over this guy. Although the program said in plain print, "no flash photography," audience members were running up to the stage to snap pictures of him. His speech rambled aimlessly from one subject to another, none of which had anything to do with our convention. That didn't matter to most of the audience, which gave him a rousing, standing ovation when his presentation finally came to a close.

A similar scene occurred at a different convention I had attended a few years earlier in Cincinnati. A former football player, a guy who actually inspired a Hollywood movie, was on our program as an alleged motivational speaker. Because of the movie, he was a hot name on the speaking circuit. For two days leading up to his speech, attendees were buzzing about this guy. They couldn't wait to see him in person and hear what pearls of wisdom he had to share with us. Finally, the moment arrived. The convention chairman read the introduction, some cheesy music played over the speakers, and the man himself, much smaller than what I had pictured, walked on stage. The crowd was practically orgasmic.

The speech stunk. It was a real clunker, utterly uninspiring to me. That didn't stop most audience members, some with tears in their eyes, from giving this guy a standing ovation. After the applause finally died down, the speaker was escorted to a table by the stage where he was available for autographs. People flocked to that autograph table like a bunch of sheep, and the line extended out the door. I was dumbfounded.

As I walked back to my hotel, I couldn't stop thinking about that long line of gushing admirers. "What was it about this guy," I wondered, "that clouded the perceptions of so many people?" The fact that he delivered a limp noodle of a speech was irrelevant to most people.

He was famous. Hollywood made a movie about him, and that was enough for the audience to give him a pass.

The smart celebrities take advantage of this and use fame to their advantage. Their fame can be parlayed into real dollars and other great benefits. Simply put, you are much more likely to be successful if a large group of people know who you are. There is nothing you can do that will change humanity's desire to worship celebrities, so you might as well take advantage of it.

BENEFITS

When it comes to making money or getting ahead in your career, there are a number of benefits to being well known. Even if it is only at a narrow, localized level, celebrity comes with benefits. Those benefits are why you must develop a high degree of name recognition.

As I've already established, celebrity will bring you admiration. Even if there are better-qualified, but lesser-known, competitors around, you will get the lion's share of the opportunities. By simply achieving strong name recognition, you are granted authority status whether you deserve it or not. That's why so many everyday people take political cues from Hollywood types, who really don't know what they're talking about.

People like to be around well-known people. It makes them feel important, influential and connected. An "A-list" party is a coveted invitation because of who is invited. Actors, musicians, big-time corporate executives, elected officials and wealthy philanthropists are constantly being invited to prestigious events because of who they are.

I recently attended a speech by Dr. Ben Bernanke, Chairman of the Federal Reserve Bank. Billionaire investor Warren Buffett attended and was seated next to Bernanke. It was an obvious seating arrangement. What event organizer wouldn't seat the nation's second richest man next the nation's most important monetary policymaker. You don't have to be as rich and famous as Warren Buffett to be a person with inside access. You just have to be a celebrity in your own sphere.

Establishing a high level of name recognition allows you to exploit one of those "80/20" rules: 20 percent of the people get 80 percent of the opportunities. I am not a famous person, but I am well known in my home base. Since becoming involved in the community, writing newspaper columns and hosting a radio show, I have established a local name for myself. That has given me far more opportunities than I would have otherwise enjoyed.

For instance, on two occasions, I had the opportunity to drive a vehicle full of government VIPs in President Bush's motorcade. By the way, that's one of the coolest things I've ever done. The vehicles drive in a line across the airport tarmac right up to Air Force One. Once the President and his entourage are loaded into their assigned vehicles, the motorcade takes off. It's the only time you get to blow down a residential street at 70 miles per hour, while running stop signs and traffic lights with police escorting you the entire way.

Simply put, you are much more likely to be successful if a large group of people know who you are.

Driving in the President's motorcade didn't necessarily boost my career, but it was a great time. I had a blast. You see many of the inside workings and the Secret Service activities that are part of a presidential visit. Had I not been well connected and known in the community, I never would have had this awesome experience.

Developing a high degree of name recognition encourages other people to talk about you. Although we often criticize name dropping as an annoying form of gossip, it is a fact of life. Go to any networking event, and you'll probably have a couple of people engaging in an impromptu name-dropping contest. Even though name droppers can be annoying, it is good to be the *subject* of name droppers. You know you're doing something right in your self marketing campaign when people are compelled to drop your name in casual conversation.

INFAMY

As much as localized fame can boost your career, infamy must be studiously avoided. Infamy can be defined as a highly public reputation for something negative. In its purest definition, the word *infamy* is reserved for people who are well known for evil or criminal acts. In modern vernacular, it can be used to describe someone who is well known but not respected. While it is good to be an effective self marketer, it is bad to be known as an infamous, self-obsessed one.

It is important to develop a level of celebrity, but make sure you become known for the right reasons. Although there's an old saying that "bad publicity is better than no publicity," you want to develop a positive name, a respected brand. A good reputation is earned through hard work, good behavior and consistent performance.

PROCRASTINATION

Don't procrastinate. You need to get started with name building now. Because it is so important to career success, some people feel as if they're not ready to build a personal brand. They think they need to be perfect at something before going out and building themselves up in public. This is a mistake. It is impossible to achieve perfection. If you wait for that, you will never get a well-known name and will thus miss out on untold opportunities.

THE COST

Becoming well known does come with a price. Before you begin pouring your time and resources into building a high degree of name recognition, you should be prepared for some changes in your life. Even local celebrity comes with challenges. Well-known people have social responsibilities. As a publicly known expert, you are being watched constantly by a large number of people. Some will admire you. Some will be jealous of you. You will have a moral obligation to set a good example, especially for young people. You will need to be positive, friendly and upbeat even when you're tired and don't feel good.

While it comes with some costs, name recognition is necessary to achieve your career potential. Just be prepared: You'll have to deal with some new issues in your life.

HOW TO BUILD NAME RECOGNITION

We have established that it all begins with name recognition. We've discussed what name recognition is, but how do you establish it? What can a typical professional do to develop it? The next several chapters answer these questions explaining how to get involved by starting within your current company, network formally and informally, harness the media, speak, write and use the Internet. It is now time to get down to the nitty-gritty. Once you understand the material in the next few chapters, you can start building the name recognition necessary to be a rock star in your own sphere of interest.

CHAPTER FIVE

Get Involved: Find Opportunities Where You Least Expect Them

E ARLY IN 2002, I ACCOMPANIED MY WIFE, STEPHANIE, TO A SOCIAL GATH-
ering at her colleague's home. I really wasn't looking forward to
the event. I wouldn't know anyone other than my wife, and I was-
n't feeling all that great. Nevertheless, sometimes you have to suck it
up and do things for your spouse. Lord knows she does that for me!

As is usually the case in such situations, the party turned out to be
much better than I had anticipated. Stephanie's colleague had a beautiful house. The appetizers were tasty and the drinks were cold. The
guests were accomplished people who engaged in interesting conversation. I enjoyed myself.

I started conversing with the colleague's wife, Michele. I discovered
she had a Ph.D. in real estate from Ohio State University and that she
was an adjunct (part-time) faculty member at the University of

Nebraska at Omaha where she taught a real estate sales and leasing course. This was interesting, because I had just recently started working in commercial real estate, and despite having spent most of my career as a college administrator, I didn't know doctoral programs in real estate even existed. With our mutual interests in real estate and academia, we had a great discussion.

Eventually, Michele suggested I visit her class as a guest lecturer. Her expertise was in residential real estate, so she wanted someone like me to discuss my experiences in commercial real estate. Not one to pass on the opportunity to share my opinion with a captive audience, I jumped at the chance.

I spoke for about an hour and was well received by the students. They paid close attention and asked good questions. Michele said she appreciated my taking time out of my busy schedule, but I was thrilled to do it. It was an enjoyable exercise for me to describe my work in a speech format, plus giving the speech was fun.

As luck would have it, Michele's husband landed a new job in Pennsylvania shortly before the start of the next semester. This prohibited her from teaching the class again. University officials were nervous about filling the teaching slot so soon before another semester. The department chair asked Michele if she knew of anyone who could take her teaching assignment. Fortunately, she thought of me. "There is a gentleman who works in commercial real estate, who spoke to my class last semester," she said. "He hasn't taught real estate before, but he has a graduate degree, served as a college dean and has taught other courses at the collegiate level."

I interviewed with the chair of the economics department, Dr. Kim Sosin, and the director of the real estate and land use economics program, Dr. Roger Sindt. The next thing I knew, I was studying textbooks, writing lecture notes and preparing for my new part-time assignment as an adjunct faculty member in UNO's College of Business Administration.

I have now completed my fifth year teaching this class. It has been a great experience – both professionally rewarding and personally enjoyable. Teaching has been advantageous for my career in many ways, and I am thankful for the opportunity. Not only is it enjoyable, it has made me much more competent. As the old saying goes, "You don't know it until you've taught it."

The academic leaders at UNO never would have hired me if they didn't believe in my competence, but I would have never been a candidate for the job had I not attended a cocktail party several months earlier. This story is a perfect example of the tremendous benefits that come from being involved. While much of this chapter will focus on professional and community involvement, even social activity is good for your career. An active social life helps you find new clients and make big deals.

SOCIAL ACTIVITY

When you are in a social setting, make it worthwhile. Too many people go to a function, grab a cocktail, hang out close to the food and speak only with people they already know. That may feel "safe," but it does not allow you to market yourself. I often go to social events by myself, so I am not tempted to huddle up with people I already know. When I attend a social event with my colleagues from Coldwell Banker Commercial World Group, we purposely split up. That way we all have to go meet new people. You never know – that stranger with whom you strike up a conversation at a reception could turn out to be a great client, a future boss or a good friend.

Many professionals are uncomfortable in social settings, especially when they don't know many other invitees. That's natural. Anytime we step out of our comfort zones, it's common to feel anxious. Deep down, I'm more introverted than extroverted, so I understand. You just have to take a deep breath and force yourself to go. Just approach a few strangers at a party and make small talk. After a while, you will get used to it, and mingling will become second nature to you.

Whether your primary involvement is social, professional or community-service oriented, you need to do something. You must lead an active life. Most of us only have about 80 to 90 years on this earth. Only 40 of those years are good income-earning years for the typical person. That means you should make every year count. You can do that by living an active, fulfilling life.

A DELIBERATE LIFE

The American philosopher Henry David Thoreau once said, "I went to the woods, because I wanted to live deliberately. I wanted to love deep and suck out all the marrow of life." I love that passage, and while I'm not hiding out on Walden Pond, I try to follow that philosophy. I can honestly say that I live my life deliberately. I made a conscious decision to be active and suck all the marrow out of life when I switched jobs and moved to a new city in 1994. I've been living accordingly ever since. Not only has that made life more interesting, it has brought great opportunities. Those opportunities are good self marketing vehicles, which of course lead to greater career success. Make no doubt about it, one of the best things you can do to promote yourself and get ahead in your career is to live life deliberately. That means you get off the couch, turn off the television and get involved.

As long as you don't over-commit yourself – burning the candle at both ends, so to speak – being involved actually makes you better at your core work. Studies have proven this.

When I worked in collegiate student affairs administration, we used to preach the merit of extracurricular activity or what we simply called "involvement." Scholars who study student success have determined that between two-thirds and three-quarters of collegiate learning takes place outside the classroom.

It's a simple fact – college students who are involved on campus are statistically much more successful academically. There are a number of reasons for this. Involved students have a greater emotional attachment to campus, so they are more likely to stick it out when things get rough. Involved students make more friends. They have more fun and they augment the things they learn in class. Involved students gain leadership experience and get an early start mastering the critically important "soft skills," such as punctuality, professionalism, interpersonal communication, for examples.

These students also have a head start on networking. College friends will someday be professional colleagues or perhaps even bosses and clients. The collegiate years are a great time for early go-getters to start building their networks. When graduation approaches, highly involved students get better jobs, bigger salaries and find employment faster than those students who focused solely on academics.

Involvement is even more important in the business world. People who join professional associations, who get involved in their place of worship, or who engage in community service learn more and meet more people. Many of the people you meet during involvement opportunities are members of your personal target audience. In any given office, there is at least one person who is active in the community and seemingly knows everyone. It is no coincidence that such a person brings in a lot of business, finds great publicity opportunities for the company and, in turn, gets a lot of promotions.

> ## Self promotion is a 24-hour-a-day, 365-days-a-year obligation.

Simply put, involvement leads to success. Self promotion is a 24-hour-a-day, 365-days-a-year obligation. It does not end until your career ends. You must be out there seeing and being seen. You have to do it perpetually, so that your personal target audience remembers you. Some people get involved and network with people extensively for a couple years, but then they kind of drift away. As time goes by, nobody thinks about them anymore. You have to stay constantly "top-of-mind" among your public. That means you get involved!

There are a number of ways to get involved, each with its advantages. What you choose to do is entirely up to you.

Chambers of Commerce

Your local chamber of commerce is a great way to get involved. In my city, the chamber is quite strong and offers approximately 100 business networking events a year. I make it a point to attend as many of these as my schedule allows. In a lot of communities, the chamber is a hub of activity and a clearinghouse of business information.

Comprised of businesses that pay yearly membership dues, chambers of commerce exist to promote economic development and help members make more money.

As an individual, you should make sure your company is a member. In many cases, the employees of member companies have access to all or most of the chamber networking opportunities.

If you are an entrepreneur and have not yet joined your local chamber, you are missing a valuable opportunity to do more business.

Being involved in my local chamber – the Greater Omaha Chamber of Commerce – has been a rewarding experience. I've been privileged to serve on a couple chamber committees, including Opportunities/Jobs/Careers, a committee dedicated to improving the local labor force. For two years, I was a steering committee member for the chamber's Young Professionals Council. Fifteen professionals, ages 25 to 40, advised chamber leadership on issues important to up-and-coming professionals. We also planned quarterly networking events and a city-wide "Young Professionals Summit" that drew 750 attendees.

A chamber of commerce may also provide an opportunity for you to deliver a presentation on your area of expertise. My chamber offers a series of educational programs known as "The Chamber Academy." These are two-hour educational sessions held once a week. The academy programs are presented by chamber members for chamber members. Attending the academies is a good way to network. Presenting at the academies builds name recognition and enhances your reputation.

On two occasions, I have been part of our chamber's annual trip to Washington, D.C. More than 100 local business leaders fly to the nation's capital to meet with members of our congressional delegation and hear briefings from administration officials about salient business issues. Although the primary missions of the trip are lobbying and education, the biggest benefits come from networking. Among the 100 professionals who participate are business owners, corporate CEOs, elected officials and other people of influence. Being confined on airplanes and buses with these decision-makers for a couple days is an absolutely incredible way to network, build name recognition and develop a respected reputation.

When colleagues ask me how they can raise their profile in the community, the first thing I tell them is go to the chamber's office. It is perhaps the easiest and most useful way for a business person to get involved.

Politics

Political parties, interest groups and election campaigns are useful ways to get involved. In politically oriented groups, you get to know people who are philosophically like-minded. Because you share a similar ideology or a passion for a given candidate or issue, the people you meet in politics tend to become good friends.

Getting involved in politics is as easy as falling off a log. There are scores of political groups advocating every possible belief you can fathom. More importantly, almost all of them are in need of more volunteers to help carry out the cause. There are never enough people around to help on campaigns or to hold leadership positions on committees. If you show up, work hard and have a positive attitude, political leaders will give you all sorts of opportunities.

To get involved in your political party, just pick up the phone. Both Republicans and Democrats have party organizations at the national, state and county levels. Within those levels are multiple committees. Furthermore, there are groups for specialized populations such as Young Republicans or College Democrats. If you call your state or county party office, someone should be able to get you started. State and local Republican and Democratic parties also hold conventions and rallies, which are ideal places to meet people.

Joining an election campaign is just as easy. Whether you want to volunteer to work for a politician running for U.S. Senate or a local school board, there are plenty of opportunities. Candidates running for big offices (Congress, governor, mayor) will most likely lease office space and have listed phone numbers for the campaign. Campaigns for some of the smaller local offices might not be as easy to find, but you should be able to track down their contact information online.

When you figure out the campaign or candidate that interests you, simply call the office and tell whoever answers that you want to volunteer. The next thing you know, they'll have you stuffing envelopes, making phone calls and marching in the Fourth of July parade. As you're doing all this, meet as many people as you possibly can. A number of these people are members of your personal target audience.

Interest groups are formed by people who are passionate about certain policy issues. These groups lobby – exert pressure on elected officials – for legislation favorable to the group's objectives. Some interest groups are industry related, others are socially focused, while still others advocate one political agenda item. Examples of interest groups are the National Rifle Association, Common Cause, Right to Life, National Association of Manufacturers, and the American Civil Liberties Union. If you feel strongly about a certain issue, there is probably a group out there where you can join your peers in advocacy of your beliefs. While you're involved in such a group and enjoying the work, just be sure to use it as a self marketing vehicle.

There are more ways to use politics for self promotion. I once testified before a committee of the state legislature that was considering a tax bill. The legislator sponsoring the bill was a friend of mine, and he asked me to come to the state capitol and help his cause. As I gave my prepared remarks, I realized what a great self-promotion opportunity it was. In addition to a direct audience of several state senators, there was an auditorium full of influential spectators.

You can also be appointed to official state boards and advisory committees by the governor of your state. Such boards are created by statute or executive order and often have a great deal of power.

As a real estate licensee, I am subject to state real estate law and the rules and regulations enforced by the real estate commission. In my state, real estate commissioners are appointed by the governor. Many other boards operate in the same way. Your fellow board members would likely be the types of people you would want to impress.

Similarly, cities have influential boards comprised of members appointed by the mayor.

If this type of involvement interests you, contact your governor's or mayor's office. Staff members can forward you an application and instructions on how to apply for an appointment. It helps if you have a relationship with the elected official or his or her top-ranking staff members.

Giving money to politicians or ballot-issue campaigns is another way you can use politics to establish name recognition. If you pay to be listed as a host or sponsor of a political fundraiser, your name will appear on the invitation, which can go out to hundreds and sometimes thousands of influential invitees. Often the cost to be listed as a host is only a little more than admission to the fundraiser.

In addition to meeting people, there is another great benefit of political involvement. As you become heavily involved in politicking, you will gain intimate knowledge of the process. As I've said before, self marketing is analogous to political campaigning. Like the politician running for office, the self-marketing professional has to have a distinguishing message, a target audience, and a communication plan. Both the politician and the self marketer must build name recognition and great reputations. If you want to borrow self marketing ideas from politicians, there is no better way than to get involved at the ground level of some local election campaign.

Working as a political volunteer now may lead to a future political candidacy for you. Most of today's political candidates started out as campaign volunteers or staffers for other politicians. As a volunteer, you can observe campaigns and candidates and learn how they really work. You can learn what candidate behaviors are helpful and harmful. Although the thought of running for office may now seem like an overwhelming impossibility, your opinion could change.

Serving as an elected official can do wonders for your career. You gain power, prestige and inside access. You become a celebrity. When you are done with your public service, you can parlay that into big executive jobs, nice consulting assignments and memberships on boards of directors.

Religion

In addition to spiritual and emotional benefits, being involved at your place of worship is another way to network and to build a good reputation. Churches and synagogues are among the most active, lively organizations on the planet.

Religious involvement feels comfortable. You are getting to know people who believe the same things you do and hold similar values. Most churches have a governance structure that allows congregants to get involved. The church may have a board of directors, church council, parish council, elders, trustees, and other officials. Under the primary legislative body of your church, there are probably many committees. Each committee is responsible for a key area of the church's mission.

For three years, I served as a member of my church's governing council. I was vice president for one of those years. Because churches fulfill an important mission, this was meaningful work, but it came with its other benefits. Church contacts can become clients and also good friends.

Religious organizations are uniquely effective in their ability to provide involvement for specific demographic groups. Examples include men's clubs, women's organizations, singles groups and youth groups. Education is a big part of life in religious organizations. Many members choose to take courses in the liturgy or traditions of the faith. Churches also put on a number of special events especially on or near religious holidays. All of these events are great ways to build personal relationships, which can be advantageous for your career.

Neighborhood Associations

Most neighborhoods have a group of activists who work together to improve quality of life in the neighborhood. Some groups are much more active than others. In some neighborhoods, the association will enforce covenants or put on special programming for kids. In other neighborhoods, the association may be focusing on cutting crime, improving parks and fixing up run-down properties.

Participating in neighborhood associations is kind of like participating in politics. The meetings often follow parliamentary procedure, and association officers are elected each year, providing leadership opportunities. Many people have successfully used neighborhood associations to launch themselves into bigger, higher-profile involvement.

Tips Clubs

In tips clubs, carefully chosen groups of professionals get together on a weekly or monthly basis to share ideas, give each other referrals and talk about rumors in the marketplace. Some tips clubs can be independent organizations, formed by one of the members. Others might be sponsored by an entity such as your local chamber of commerce. There are nationally organized tips clubs with local chapters all over the country. A great example is BNI International, the largest business networking organization in the world. BNI has chapters around the world. Large U.S. cities will have multiple chapters.

In most tips clubs only one member is allowed from any one industry area. That means there will be only one accountant, attorney, construction contractor, real estate agent or financial planner per tip group. That way, members can say what they want without worrying about a direct competitor being in the room. In order for tips clubs to work properly, they require a major commitment: You can't miss many meetings, and you have to bring a tip or referral to each meeting. A tip would be inside information or a well-founded rumor that you think most, or all, of your fellow tips club members would not know. A referral would be a business lead for another member.

Kids

If you are a parent or grandparent, chances are you spend quite a bit of time at soccer games, baseball practices and piano recitals. While supporting your progeny, you can also be doing business. I know of several dads who have done business deals while chatting with other dads along the soccer sideline at the neighborhood park. Kids also make a great excuse. If your child's playmate has a parent you would like to meet, set up a time for the kids to play and for you to network with an important member of your personal target audience.

Another way you can exploit your parental status for self marketing purposes is to get involved in school organizations, such as the Parent-Teacher Association. Schools have committees of parents and community volunteers that help with a variety of functions. Although my son, Jack, is a few years away from starting school, I am serving on the communications advisory board for the Millard Public Schools. We meet quarterly to give our input on how the district's policies and actions affect external relations. The committee is made up of parents and members of the local media. It's always a good idea to build relationships with members of the media.

Service Clubs

Rotary, Kiwanis, Sertoma and Optimists are examples of international service clubs that have local chapters in almost every significantly sized town in America. Service clubs have strict membership requirements and expect members to be active. Meetings take place regularly, often every week. Some clubs charge you a fine if you miss too many meetings. Each service club focuses on a charity. Much of the programming and fundraising that the club undertakes is geared toward helping a targeted group of needy people.

Aside from benefiting your community and your fellow human beings, service-club membership is a great way to get involved. Service club members tend to be educated, somewhat affluent and well connected. These organizations elect officers, thus providing leadership opportunities for their members. There are also regional and national conventions that allow you to network with like-minded people in other cities.

Fraternal Organizations

Fraternal organizations are somewhat similar to service clubs. The term *fraternal* implies a sense of brotherhood. Ideally, members think of themselves as de facto brothers or sisters.

On college campuses, fraternities and sororities usually are named after letters in the Greek alphabet. Collegiate fraternities and sororities have alumni organizations to satisfy those members who want lifelong involvement. While in college, I was a member of Tau Kappa Epsilon fraternity. Unfortunately, I haven't found the time to be involved as an alumnus, but some of the guys my age still are.

Fraternal organizations open to professionals occasionally have Greek letters, but many do not. Examples of fraternal organizations include the Freemasons, Knights of Columbus, Ancient Order of Hibernians, B'nai Brith and the Elks Club.

Philanthropy

Many of the social elites enjoy participating in charitable causes. Although some people engage in charity just to get their pictures in the society magazines, most do it to make the world a better place while having a good time. In philanthropic involvement, groups usually throw a big party, ball or gala with the proceeds going to a chosen charity. Admission to some of these shindigs can be quite pricey. Tuxedos and formal gowns are costly too. Many of these events will include auctions to further raise money. Bidding on sale items will obviously increase your monetary outlay. To cut your personal costs, you should see if your company will pay for part or all of your participation in these events.

Philanthropic organizations and the charities they serve usually have boards of directors, advisory panels and planning committees. Be careful, however, that you don't just join boards to pad your resumé. If you join, you will be expected to contribute your time and talent. Some of the larger, more prestigious charitable organizations will expect each board member to make a financial contribution or at least raise a minimum amount of money.

Philanthropic events tend to draw a higher socio-economic crowd – the types of people who can send you business or who could do things for your career. Those self marketers who are not used to societal events may be a little intimidated by the formality and the occasional show of wealth. Don't let that stop you from including philanthropy as one of the methods you use to get involved and market yourself.

Philanthropy is a name-recognition builder. Often donors are listed on event programs, newsletters and annual reports. Large donors may be listed on permanent plaques. It pays to get on these lists. Anytime we see a list of people who donate money, we naturally look to see if we know anyone. The more you show up on the lists, the more people will remember you.

If you don't have a lot of money, be strategic about choosing your charities. Donate just enough to get on the list and go for the higher profile organizations.

Professional Associations

Whether you work in accounting, human resources or civil engineering, there are professional associations available for you to join. Professional associations bring people of one discipline together for educational and networking purposes. These groups can be very specialized.

When I was dean of student services at Clarkson College, I belonged to the National Association of College Admissions Counseling and the American Association of Collegiate Registrars and Admissions Officers. It doesn't get much more specialized than that! Both of these organizations hold national conventions each year, drawing thousands of conventioneers. Many professional associations are national or international in scope but offer involvement in state and local chapters.

From a self marketing perspective, professional associations are additional ways to advance your career. By taking a leadership role in one of these organizations, you have the chance to impress people in your field of expertise. That could lead to a new job at a competing company. Because the programming provided by professional associations helps you be more competent in your job, there is a good chance that your current employer will pay for part or all of the costs associated with belonging to these groups.

Back to School

After working in the corporate world for several years, my wife enrolled in a Master of Business Administration degree program. She worked during the day and took classes at night. During the two-and-a-half years it took her to earn the MBA, she was able to meet several interesting people and network with professionals from other companies. As part of the curriculum, she took a 10-day trip to Ireland with her classmates. It was a bonding experience, and although she completed the program a few years ago, several of her cohorts remain close friends.

Enrolling in graduate school or resuming work on an unfinished baccalaureate degree are both great ways to get involved, while enhancing your knowledge and capabilities. Business educational programs are especially valuable, because business-college pedagogy employs a lot of group work, forcing you to get to know your classmates. Additionally, the types of people enrolled in business programs are likely successful decision makers or at least future decision makers.

The Arts

Most major cities have a plethora of artistic involvement opportunities. You could choose to be a volunteer tour guide at an art museum or an usher during shows at your local performing arts center.

If you can act, local theater productions are a way to meet people while getting your name in front of the public. Local, non-professional theaters commonly announce their auditions in newspapers or online and open them to the public. Until you get a little more experienced in the theater world, you probably won't land the leading lady's role, but any part can get you exposed while allowing you to develop friendships with your fellow actors.

Music is another great way to get involved. A tremendous number of American kids take vocal or instrumental music classes in grade school and high school. Most of these kids hang up the instrument once they graduate. If you have some musical ability and don't want it to simply fade away, there are numerous bands, choirs or other performance groups that will allow you to pursue an enjoyable hobby while establishing name recognition.

Sports and Recreation

Like the performing arts, most of us have participated in sports during our younger years. There's no reason you have to be put out to athletic pasture once your school days are over. Many professionals participate in amateur athletic leagues to stay in shape, have fun and perhaps, most important, get involved. From sand volleyball at a local sports bar to softball and bowling leagues, there is no limit to the sports and recreational involvement options. There's a good chance your city has large organizations that exist solely to provide adults with the opportunity to compete and have a great time meeting others.

Special Events

Each June, my hometown hosts the National Collegiate Athletic Association's College World Series, the national championship for men's baseball. Thousands of baseball fans descend on Omaha's Rosenblatt Stadium for this 10-day celebration of America's pastime. It's a huge event, one which requires a great deal of volunteer help. Many local residents help out each year. Perhaps they just love baseball, but most people do it as a way to get involved in something exciting.

Every city has special events. Whether it's the annual marathon, an outdoor summer concert series, or the city's anniversary celebration, a number of major events require a lot of volunteers. By getting involved, you meet people, promote yourself among other go-getters and have fun doing it.

Awards and Recognition

After you successfully become involved, you may be in line for awards and recognition. Although it may seem self-serving, savvy self marketers seek out awards. It's not about ego; it's about earning name recognition and building a positive reputation.

I haven't received a large number of awards in my life, but a few years ago I received a very nice one that had a beneficial effect on my career. A local business newspaper recognized me as one of the 40 outstanding business leaders under age 40. I truly appreciated the award. It came with a handsome wall plaque and a lengthy write-up and picture when the award was granted. Later in the year, the newspaper ran a personality-profile article on me. You can't buy that kind of positive publicity.

Awards are so helpful in boosting your name recognition that they are worth striving for even if you have to fill out an application and go through an interview.

We once had a real estate agent who did some graphic design and marketing work for us on the side. She was quite talented and produced high-quality printed materials. An invitation she created for one of our broker open houses was particularly attractive. She entered it into a design contest sponsored by a local marketing association. She was quite pleased when her piece won top prize in its category, bringing well-deserved attention to her skills and ability. She established name recognition and furthered her reputation in the marketing industry.

THE BENEFITS

In addition to building name recognition and ultimately marketing yourself, getting involved has other benefits. For one thing, involvement helps you develop a personal information trail. In other words, the more you do in the community and in your profession, the more likely your name is to pop up on lists, databases and on the Internet. When I want to find out about a given person, I "Google" them. If the person's name shows up on a lot of websites, I'm impressed.

In a crowded, competitive and noisy global marketplace, self marketing is critical. One of the ways you market yourself is by creating a personal trail on the Internet. Any time you join a group or get involved in a cause, you may get your name on another website.

To find out how widespread your name is on the World Wide Web, I recommend you go "ego surfing" once a month. Simply Google your own name and notice where it pops up. If you don't see your name a lot, it's a sign that you may not be getting a big enough benefit from your current involvement.

Getting involved often allows you to do interesting things that your typical couch potato never experiences. My company has a membership in the local chapter of Building Owners and Managers Association. I occasionally go to BOMA meetings. A few years ago, during a BOMA meeting, we had the opportunity to take a service elevator to the 40th floor of a skyscraper that was under construction. The floor was in place but no walls were present. I could walk to the edge of the 40th floor and only two cables, crafted into a sort of "fence," separated me from a 600-foot death dive. As a real estate guy, I love tall buildings, and I love construction. For me, it was incredibly cool to put on a hard hat and spend a half hour on the highest floor-plate of an unfinished skyscraper. Had my company not been involved in BOMA, I would have never done that.

Involvement makes you wiser. It is one of the best educational opportunities available. That's important, because in today's technological economy, we must be constantly learning. We must stay on the cutting edge. Getting involved helps you do just that. Like college students, we professionals learn more in out-of-the-office involvement than we do while performing our basic, core job functions.

EVERYWHERE!

An acquaintance of mine, who runs an event planning business, recently noticed my quote and picture in a newspaper article on real estate development. A week earlier, she saw me do an interview on television. Furthermore, she occasionally listened to my radio show. She would frequently see me at networking functions around town. She called me one afternoon and said, "I just have to tell you – you are *everywhere!*" She was amazed at how well I was getting around town, meeting people and building my name recognition. I told her it was just part of my job as vice president and part of my long-term strategy for a successful career. I wasn't telling her anything she didn't already know, because she too did a darned good job getting around town.

Use your time wisely. If you have family or other commitments in the evening, make sure you use your lunch hour for networking and other self marketing activities. Ambitious professionals should not eat lunch by themselves more than once a week; it's simply too important of a networking opportunity to waste.

The fact is, in order to stand out, you need to be everywhere. As much as you may desire to go home and watch television after work, you need to spend a little more time working, showing up at events. My boss jokingly tells our real estate agents, "You have to sacrifice your liver to make it in this business." In other words, you've got to be out socializing and schmoozing people if you want to get clients and do deals. While you don't have to drink until your liver gives out, you do need to be a man or woman about town. Sometimes you have to stay out late at a cocktail party where important prospects have gathered. Sometimes you need to get up early and meet a member of your personal target audience for coffee before you both start work.

It's not easy, and it comes with a price, but big-time, successful professionals are seemingly "everywhere." There's no doubt about it: To get ahead you need to get involved.

CHAPTER SIX

Start Self Marketing Inside Your Current Company

WHEN STARTING ANY NEW ENDEAVOR, IT ONLY MAKES SENSE TO PICK THE low-hanging fruit first. In the self marketing game, there's a lot of low-hanging fruit in your current place of employment. While much of this book is focused on marketing yourself to the greater world, it is important to remember that the easiest and most logical place to start is right under your nose.

It doesn't cost you much to focus your self marketing inside your current company. Many professionals work for huge organizations that are full of talented, motivated and highly successful people. In these situations, you have hundreds of personal target audience members right beside you, collecting paychecks from the same entity that gives you yours.

Companies are microcosms of the global economy. They are subcultures of the broader community. They are ideal places to hone your professional and self marketing skills before announcing yourself to a bigger marketplace. It is much easier to become a rock star inside one company than it is to become one in a whole city or the entire country.

You can adopt a number of behaviors to maximize your self-marketing opportunities at work. First and foremost, you simply need to be a good person. The old saying "nice guys finish last" is not true. To get ahead in today's world you need to be nice and not just nice to your boss and the higher ups. If you are consistently nice to everyone in the company, you will build a stellar reputation. Being nice does not mean that you become a pushover. On the contrary, having a reputation for treating people well will make others pay attention much more closely when you do have to make bold decisions that make some people unhappy.

You need to build relationships with your colleagues. You don't necessarily want to be known as the company partier who gets blasted drunk with co-workers every night after work. You do want to have healthy professional relationships with people at work. In fact, recent research by the Gallup Organization has shown that people who have a "best friend" at work tend to be happier, more effective and stay with the company longer. Solid work relationships enrich your career and make your job more fun. They are also useful when you need allies during one of those institutional political struggles that companies deal with periodically.

ASSERTIVE, AGGRESSIVE, PASSIVE

One of the best things you can do to market yourself inside your company is to adopt a positive attitude. This is critically important, because nobody likes being around negative people. Positive behavior means that you understand the difference among the words, *aggressive, assertive* and *passive*. In the professional setting, assertiveness is good. Aggression and passivity are bad. Aggression makes you overbearing and turns people off. If you choose to be aggressive at work, you will win some battles, but you'll fail in the career-long pursuit of true excellence. People avoid aggressive colleagues and work around them, finding ways to isolate them and keep them out of the loop.

People tend to disrespect or pity passive employees. Anyone with career ambitions needs to avoid passivity. In addition to being run over by more aggressive colleagues, passive people can give the impression that they are uninterested, not curious and not proactive. Most passive people are not actually this way; they just appear that way to others.

Passive-aggressiveness is another behavior trait that should be studiously avoided. Passive-aggressive people tend to say one thing even though they mean another. This behavior shows up often in personal relationships. For example, one spouse might suggest a certain restaurant for dinner. The other spouse, says, "Sure. That's fine, I suppose." During dinner, the spouse that said it's okay becomes the passive-aggressive one by playing with their food, looking away all the time and not engaging in conversation. In the professional world, passive-aggressive people tend to pout, allow bad things to happen and sometimes deliberately sabotage things. Being passive-aggressive is one of the easiest ways to get fired.

Assertiveness is healthy; it's a balance between aggressive and passive behavior. Assertive people don't let anyone take advantage of them, but they are not overbearing. They give credit where credit is due, but they are not shy about accepting praise when they deserve it. Assertive professionals have goals and work hard to accomplish them. They know that they need other people in order to get ahead. They employ others without exploiting them. Assertive people focus more on the work at hand and less on the behavior or personality weaknesses of the people around them. Essentially, all the legitimate techniques you can use to promote yourself inside your company come down to assertiveness: good, healthy, balanced, professional behavior.

BE A SOLUTION PERSON

So, what are some ways you can exhibit healthy, assertive behavior inside your current company? To start, be a solution person. In our post-modern world, the people with great ideas and answers to complicated questions are the ones who bring value to a workplace. The more value you bring, the better your reputation. Even when you are frustrated with the direction your company is going, and you're considering pursuing other opportunities, you need to keep up a positive attitude and always contribute solutions to problems. Too many professionals fall into the short-term-thinking trap. Don't let that happen to you. Everything you do at your current place of employment has an effect on your future. That means you must constantly strive to find solutions up to your last day in a given job.

As a solution person, you are always looking to create something or discover something. To build the best possible reputation at your current company, you need to be vigilantly on the lookout for new ideas. You always want something of value you can bring to the table. Do your research. Think creatively and try to come up with the next great thing that will make your company money.

There's the catch, however: No matter how hard you work being innovative and creative, you have to share your information. Hoarding information doesn't cut it. If you keep your information secret, it won't be of benefit to the company, and it won't help you market yourself and build up a great image at work. Sharing ideas with the team is a healthy, assertive form of behavior. People in your immediate group or department will know the ideas are yours. With colleagues outside your immediate department, you can subtly mention that you came up with the idea.

GIVING CREDIT TO OTHERS

Speaking of sharing, it is critical that you share credit. This is especially important if you have people working for you. Publicly, smart leaders give the credit to their subordinates and take responsibility when someone under their leadership screws up. This makes you look good over the long run and builds loyalty among your troops. President Abraham Lincoln, a masterful leader, knew well the importance of this philosophy. He understood that boosting egos of those who reported to him boosted productivity, making him ultimately more successful. He knew that absorbing blame when things went badly strengthened the bond between the subordinate and him, fostering a strong sense of loyalty. As Lincoln knew so well, you get ahead much faster if the people around you love and respect you more than you do if they are intimidated by you.

While pursuing my master's degree, I was fortunate to have a graduate assistantship. In exchange for free tuition, I worked 20 hours a week in student affairs administration. During this time, I worked for Patrick McBride, a textbook example of a great boss. Pat thoroughly understood and lived by Abraham Lincoln's management principles. He shared the credit and absorbed the blame. He truly empowered his employees to make decisions at the lowest level and encouraged us to take on extra responsibility. Because Pat's management philosophy was so supportive, employees felt safe to take risks. That led to a creative, entrepreneurial spirit that was frankly not present in a lot of other offices inside a large university bureaucracy. This mentality has fostered tremendous loyalty among Pat's staff past and present.

I haven't worked for Pat since 1993, but to this day, I appreciate the things he taught me. His staff has always been widely admired and respected throughout the university and his reputation is well known. Giving credit to the people who work for him has not taken anything away from him. On the contrary, it has won him high praise and admiration.

STRONG RELATIONSHIPS

Building strong relationships inside your current company should not be limited to your boss or your direct reports. You need to interact with everyone. One way to build goodwill at work is to send periodic notes or emails, complimenting colleagues on a job well done or congratulating them on some accomplishment. Simply remembering a co-worker's birthday or the anniversary of their hiring can get you a lot of mileage.

A great opportunity occurs every time a new person starts working at your company. As you know, the first couple days on a new job can be intimidating and emotionally draining. A new employee could have a bit of "buyer's remorse" about the job or may have longings for his or her previous job. Starting a new job can be stressful and overwhelming as the neophyte tries to learn new jargon, new policies and new institutional norms. This is the opportune time for the savvy self marketer to make a valuable connection. You should go out of your way to meet new colleagues and make them feel welcome. If you take time out of your busy schedule to do this, you will likely build a strong relationship and gain an ally.

You never know – the person below you today could be your boss in five to 10 years.

You can never have too many friends in the business world. Being among the first to make a new colleague feel welcome creates a win-win situation – you have an ally indebted to you, while the new employee gets a head start and feels better about the new place of employment. Everyone's productivity likely will increase.

If you have a high-ranking position in the company, you can benefit greatly by reaching out to those who have "lesser" jobs. This type of self marketing effort not only has short-term benefits, it could have some long-term ones as well. You never know – the person below you today could be your boss in five to 10 years.

Whether a person is above you, below you or on the same level, you should go out of your way to extend courtesies. For instance, it pays to go to someone else's office or cubicle for a meeting. Don't always expect others to come to your office. By simply volunteering right off the bat to go to someone else's office, you send the message that you are unpretentious and accommodating.

Along these lines, face-to-face meetings are more effective than email and telephone communication (unless it is a mundane, routine matter). For important conversations, go and meet with someone in person. This will make a positive impression especially if you are higher up on the corporate food chain. This is especially effective if you have to discuss something the person won't like.

I also like to meet in person with those colleagues who are notoriously "difficult." Surely all of us have worked with at least one person who was obnoxious, self-absorbed, non-communicative or passive-aggressive. If you have to do business with a person like this, it works better if you show up at his or her office in person.

AVOIDING GOSSIP

Gossip is one of the biggest threats to career success. Gossip is an insidious behavior, which reflects the simplicity of the gossiper's brain. Intellectual people prefer to discuss ideas and philosophies; simple people spend their time discussing other people. Not only can gossip tear apart a department or an entire company, it reflects badly on the gossiper. I don't think a lot of gossips realize this, but they are roundly disrespected by their co-workers, who see right through it. In fact, many co-workers will actually engage periodically with a big gossiper but still look down on the person for doing it more often.

I can think of times in my career in which gossip has caused harm for the office as well as for the individual purveyors of gossip.

Against my better judgment, I once hired a woman back in my days as a college administrator. On paper, this person was the ideal candidate. Looking back, I may have decided subconsciously to hire her just because I was so impressed with the words written on her resumé. When she showed up for the interview, she had the right "look" – well dressed, a put-together professional image, which only reinforced my preconceived notions of her. She was confident and polished to the point that she immediately impressed me. During the interview, however, I sensed a bit of sarcasm and cynicism in her personality. This would normally be a red flag; however, I chose to ignore it. That turned out to be a critical mistake.

Within days of starting employment, she was raking up muck. She gossiped with all her fellow employees, criticized everything and repeatedly stabbed all of us in the back, whenever the situation was psychologically appealing to her. Things got worse. She schmoozed the college president, manipulating him, and thus causing some friction between my boss and me. That made it even harder to get rid of her. When I finally expunged her from my department, things got a lot better, but the damage she inflicted took months to repair. In the long run, her behavior hurt her. Few people in the organization respected her, because most were able to see right through her façade and accurately assess the type of person she really was.

As you consciously avoid gossip, it is also important to practice excellent communication techniques. Among other things, this means you never blind-side your boss or a colleague. If you know of something that could embarrass or cause stress for your boss or colleagues, tell them immediately. Although they may not like hearing what you have to say, they will appreciate your honesty and helpfulness in the long run. If you lead employees, I believe you should extend them the same courtesy. Nobody likes to look stupid by being caught off guard. People will love you if you help them avoid such situations.

INDISPENSABILITY

Smart employees build themselves up by making themselves "indispensable" to their bosses. These employees learn everything they can and do important, mission-critical work with a positive attitude. If you exhibit this behavior, you will gain job security and probably more money. Even though it makes it painful for your employer when you leave, being indispensable in your current company makes you more desirable for other employers.

Sometimes, self marketers have to give subtle reminders to their bosses about their indispensable status. This is fine as long as it is done tactfully and not too often. It is also useful to have one of your colleagues reinforce your indispensability in front of the boss.

TEAM PLAYER

Being a team player does wonders for your career now and in the future. From the company's perspective, team players are good for the bottom line. From your personal perspective, it earns you respect and promotions. It also makes you look good to people outside the company. Of course, that can lead to new opportunities. Team players have a positive attitude. They are willing to try new things, and they support management's decisions. They may disagree with an idea while it's being debated, but they publicly support decisions once they are final.

Team players go out of their way to help their colleagues and the company's clients. They are supportive of their colleagues' endeavors. They encourage their colleagues to excel and are honestly happy when their co-workers succeed. They celebrate their co-workers' successes. They are good listeners and have well-developed interpersonal skills.

As a team player, you show your support by attending company events. Whether it's a summer picnic or the annual holiday party, team players show up with a positive attitude and enjoy themselves. Just be sure to behave at these company events. Many careers have been damaged by poor behavior at a company Christmas party. Although indiscretions at these company celebrations can in rare cases lead to termination, most are at least a little embarrassing.

I once worked at a small private college. There was a quasi-retired woman who served as a part-time admissions counselor in our office. She was quite a character — brilliant, diverse, cosmopolitan, a bit obnoxious in a lovable sort of way and absolutely hilarious. She had a hot-and-cold relationship with the boss. Sometimes the friction between them got a little hot.

At the college's annual holiday party, this woman appeared to be loosening up and having a great time. At the end of the dinner, the president of the college held an award ceremony recognizing the work of several staff members, including our boss. As our boss walked to the stage, my free-spirited co-worker yelled at the top of her lungs: "Asshole, Asshole!" The boss either didn't hear it, or chose to ignore it, because this woman kept her job. Unfortunately, about 20 college employees did hear it, and, by Monday, the entire faculty and staff knew about it. As you work hard to build a professional image at work, don't let one night of indiscretion permanently tarnish it.

Team players volunteer to take on extra duties and projects. This simply makes you look good and also exposes you to people in other parts of the company. In other words, as you are helping out by taking on extra responsibilities, you gain personally as well. When I was working as dean of student services, the president asked me to be the college's point person for the annual United Way drive. When you hold a leadership position, you say "yes" when the president asks you to do such things. Sure it was extra work, but it was a rewarding experience. It allowed me to work with every employee in the organization – something I didn't regularly get to do.

START AN ORGANIZATION

In some situations, you could have the opportunity to start a club or organization inside your company. As part of my responsibilities as a radio talk-show host, I give a number of speeches each year to a wide variety of clubs and organizations. I was once asked to speak to a group of Jaycees at Mutual of Omaha, a *Fortune 500* insurance company.

Mutual employs about 5,000 people on its headquarters campus, and many of them are young professionals. I was surprised to find out that this chapter of Jaycees was comprised entirely of Mutual employees. They held their meetings during the lunch hour in one of the company's training classrooms. The chapter's officers were strong leaders who ran a very active group of Jaycees.

I was amazed that a club could be entirely contained within one company. It's an innovative idea that provides mutually beneficial results for both the company and the participating employees. The employees don't have to go far to participate in an extracurricular activity. The company benefits because it fosters company loyalty and builds strong bonds among colleagues. If you work for a company large enough to support such an internal organization, perhaps you could start it. If you pull it off, you will have added something wonderful to your resumé and will have impressed numerous colleagues

CONFLICTS OF INTEREST

There's an old saying: "You shouldn't fish off the company wharf." Typically, this saying is used to discourage people from dating fellow employees, but it can apply to any potential conflict of interest. The work world presents many tempting situations. It is always wise to avoid anything that even remotely smells fishy. If you are ever tempted to get involved in a potential conflict of interest, just walk away. Remember that no short-term gain is worth jeopardizing your job.

Along those lines, be honest even when no one knows you're being honest. I once had a boss who was so focused on being 100 percent honest that he would walk across the street to the convenience store's public copy machine rather than make even one personal copy at the office. He truly believed that living a life of complete integrity was critical to career success. He's enjoying a successful career, so he may be right. If nothing else, he is able to sleep at night knowing that he never cheats anyone.

OPEN DOORS

Don't burn bridges and don't close doors. You never know when you are going to cross paths again with one of your co-workers or an old boss. It is also possible that someone who reports to you today could offer you a job at some point in the future. It is important to market yourself to everyone at every point in time. When you are leaving a company, try to leave on the best terms possible even if you are ticked off at the boss, feel unappreciated or dislike half your co-workers. Give proper notice and try not to leave things undone.

When one of your staff members or colleagues leaves the company, be sure to wish them well. If appropriate, volunteer to be a professional reference for them in the future. In my experience people really appreciate such an offer. I have former staff members from many years ago who still use me as a reference. It's a good way for me to stay in their minds. You never know: One of my former employees could end up being a client some day or could give me a great idea.

Don't assume you will never again deal with a colleague who is moving to a different city. The global economy has made the world a shockingly small place. There is a decent chance that a departing person could come back into your life. Don't let good business relationships die.

EXPLOITING YOUR COMPANY

Often when we hear the word *exploit,* it is uttered in a negative tone of voice. That doesn't have to be the case. Savvy self marketers serve their current employer while using it as an opportunity to boost themselves in the broader marketplace. If any part of your job is public, use it to your advantage. If there are internal involvement opportunities at your company, take them.

Keep in mind that the most important component of self marketing is establishing name recognition. Get your name printed and spoken any way you can. Find ways to be listed on the company website. If you are responsible for representing your company on an external project, find ways to meet as many people as possible and spread your name around in creative ways. For instance, anytime you meet with a client, give that person some basic information on your company including your bio. This will seem very normal to the client, and by doing this, the possibility exists that a client will read your bio, be impressed with you, remember you and perhaps offer you a great opportunity someday.

If you work for a small company, it should be easy to get your name on the company website and included in some of the company promotional materials. Send letters and emails to clients anytime you can think of an excuse. Hand your business card out to as many people as you can. Keep your eyes open and be creative – anytime there is a way to further your company's mission while getting your name out in public, take it!

MOVING UP ON THE JOB

Generally, it is easier to be promoted from within than it is to find a job with an entirely new company. That alone is reason enough to market yourself inside your current company. I was promoted from within twice at Clarkson College, once from assistant director to director of enrollment management, then three years later to dean of student services. These promotions came about from good performance but also from self marketing.

When I became dean, I was only 29 years old. A different college, where the leadership didn't know my personality and abilities, would not have considered such an inexperienced person for the job. When self marketing in your current company, it is easy to become obsessed with external opportunities, especially if you're not tight with your current boss. Nevertheless, keep looking for better opportunities right where you are. Internal opportunities make for easier transitions.

YOUR ETHICAL OBLIGATION

Most of my focus this chapter has been to market *yourself* inside your company in order to achieve some *personal* gain. You also have a moral duty to use your accomplishments to boost your current employer. All worthy professionals have an ethical duty to market their employer's brand at every possible opportunity. If you are at a party, you have a duty to talk up your company. Even if you don't work directly in sales, marketing or public relations, you have an obligation to promote the company.

As a professional, you are on duty 24 hours a day. When I go to a chamber of commerce event or a political fundraiser, I have a strong desire to promote myself. However, I also have a strong desire to promote my place of employment, find new clients and discover new sources of revenue. I work hard to build up the name "Jeff Beals." Much of that is for my personal benefit, but while I'm collecting a paycheck from Coldwell Banker Commercial World Group, I have a duty to use my widely recognized name and established reputation to help my company make more money.

CHAPTER SEVEN

You're Not the Average Joe: Leveraging Formal Networking

W HEN I WAS A SENIOR IN COLLEGE, I SET UP A SERIES OF ONE-ON-ONE meetings with accomplished individuals who worked for companies that interested me. Like many soon-to-graduate college students, I wasn't entirely sure what I would end up doing. I was thinking about doing something in marketing and communications, but I wasn't sure (I ended up going to graduate school instead of finding a job).

A friend of mine had just attended a career seminar at the student union. The speaker encouraged college students to develop a list of people in interesting career fields. The next steps were to contact these people, set up meetings and learn from their experience while hopefully making a positive impression. It seemed like a terrific idea to me.

I looked up several companies in a handful of industries that appealed to me. I then proceeded to identify individual professionals who held significant positions in these companies. Finding this information was a lot of work, because the Internet was not available at that time. Once I found a targeted person at the company, I wrote a letter asking for a meeting and then followed up via telephone the next week. I played up my college-student status to the hilt ("Surely you can take just a few minutes to help out a college kid who hopes someday to be just like you!").

I set up four of these appointments. Two stand out in my mind. One was an executive with a large advertising agency, and the other was the public relations director for a minor-league professional sports team. Neither meeting led to a job opportunity. I never ended up working for an ad agency or professional sports team; however, both meetings were tremendously valuable experiences.

Ten years later, when I was interested in leaving college administration and finding a job in the for-profit sector, I did the same thing. At that time, I hired a company to coach me in my job search. Interestingly, one of their key recommendations was to set up one-on-one informational interviews with targeted decision makers. Like I did as a college student, I searched companies and names of people who would be worth meeting. I met with a real estate developer, a couple business owners and several other professionals.

This second round of formal networking meetings opened my eyes and gave me a deeper understanding of several career fields. By its very nature, formal networking is artificial. If you are not prepared for the artificiality of it, and you don't go into it with a positive attitude, it could turn out to be an awkward, and therefore ineffective, situation.

PURPOSE OF FORMAL NETWORKING

Before you go to the time and trouble of setting up meetings with influential people, establish some goals. Decide what you want to get out of your formal networking efforts.

The primary reason for formal networking is to get a job or discover new opportunities. Some may do this to learn about a different industry before investing in it or going back to school to be educated in it. Another purpose of formal networking is to practice interviewing. Because the meetings are somewhat analogous to job interviews, they give you a chance to sharpen your interviewing skills without a job hanging in the balance. And because it's a low-stakes situation, you don't have much to lose but a heck of a lot to gain.

As I mentioned, most people who engage in formal networking do so for career advancement purposes. The vast majority of jobs are never advertised. These jobs are created specifically for well-suited people, or are given to someone who knows the right person. Many other jobs are internal promotions. Since the average Joe has no way of knowing about these jobs, you've got to do things that make you anything but average. You've got to tap into the job "grapevine." You've got to meet with the right people who could be impressed with you so much that they would customize a job for you.

That's what formal networking is all about. If you meet with enough people and impress them in the right way, eventually someone will create a job for you. I know this works. My most recent jobs were created for me. When I was working as director of enrollment management at Clarkson College, my boss decided that all student affairs administrative functions should be combined under one person's leadership. Fortunately, that person was me.

A few years later, I was able to enter the commercial real estate field because a good friend of mine owned a company, and he needed an administrator to help him run it. We have hired a couple of people at Coldwell Banker Commercial World Group simply because we were impressed with their skills, attitude and work ethic. Almost every company I know of does the same thing from time to time.

HOW DOES IT WORK?

The first step to using formal networking as a self marketing tool is to take a deep breath and relax. Yes, that's right: First you need to get in the right frame of mind. For some people, the idea of calling someone out of the blue to ask for a meeting is intimidating. It doesn't have to be. In my business, I am constantly calling people and inviting them to go to lunch or coffee to discuss business. The vast majority of the people I invite say "yes." What's more, I am constantly calling influential people and asking them to be guests on my radio show. Only about 2 percent of all the potential radio show guests I've called have ever said "no." Don't worry about rejection – just contact people you would like to meet. Don't worry about feeling stupid – you never look as awkward and unconfident as you fear you do.

The second step is to identify an industry or career field that interests you. Do some research and find a few companies that impress you. Thoroughly search each company's website. In addition to general information, you want to find people of influence in each company. Once you have identified who in the company you would like to meet, copy their contact information (usually available on the company website) and enter it into your personal contact database.

Next, you should draft a formal business letter requesting a short meeting. In the letter, stress that you simply are seeking an informational session and that you are NOT asking for a job interview. Furthermore, stress that you do not expect the person to even know about any possible job openings. You simply want to learn from the person's success.

Most people are kind enough to take a few minutes to help out someone thinking about entering the industry. If kindness doesn't convince the influential person, their ego might get you the meeting if you take the time to butter them up a little. In the letter, be sure to mention that you will be calling soon to set up a mutually agreeable time to meet. Please note that you can skip the letter-writing step if you have a relationship with the person or if you get a referral from a person that you and the targeted person both know personally.

After the person has received the letter, call. Although you might be tempted to procrastinate on this, don't. The longer you wait to make that call, the harder it will be psychologically. When you call, there's a good chance you will run into one of the most common roadblocks in the formal networking game: the diligent secretary.

When I call CEOs or other especially influential people to be guests on my radio show, I usually have to fight through the suspicious, gate-keeping secretary. Some secretaries are particularly difficult to crack, but none of them is foolproof. You just have to say the right things with confidence and be persistent.

Secretaries block access in a number of ways. They could say the boss is simply not interested in meeting you. They could claim the boss doesn't take any appointments. Some secretaries may simply tell you not to waste your time because the company is not hiring. Secretaries will want to know exactly who you are and why you are calling, and then once you tell them, they think of an excuse as to why you can't see your targeted big shot. Regardless of the blocking tactic employed by a given secretary, you need to bust through it.

If a secretary says, "We got your letter, but he's not hiring right now," simply repeat what you said in the letter: "I'm not looking for a job interview; I just want to ask him a few questions in order to learn about his experience and success." Keep repeating your purpose and be insistent until you are transferred to your targeted person or until the secretary agrees to book you on the boss's calendar. If the secretary drills you with questions, honesty is generally the best answer. Just explain that you are thinking about entering a new career field and that you are in the research stage. Tell the secretary you have tremendous respect for the company and the boss in particular.

If you are persistent, eventually, most secretaries either will schedule you or transfer you to the boss. Once you speak to the boss, you may have to go through the same justification process.

Generally, most people who reach a position in life where they are influential enough for an outsider to target have at least some ego. Most have a hell of a lot of ego. Play to it! The more you can stroke them, without looking too obvious, the quicker you'll get a meeting.

I know it works. I probably meet with a dozen people each year who call me requesting a meeting to discuss commercial real estate. Some find me through the company website, while others hear my radio show or read my newspaper columns. Regardless of how they find me, I'm not going to turn down someone who respectfully calls on me to provide them some basic information about the wonderful world of commercial real estate.

THE MEETING

Once you have a meeting established, you need to treat it like you would treat an actual job interview. First of all, dress in full business attire. That means you wear a business suit. Even if the company is famously casual, you should still show up to this meeting in business attire. It shows that you are serious and that you respect the company and the person. Just like an interview, you want to make sure you are on time. Show up at the office a few minutes before the scheduled meeting time. Once you arrive, be very professional to the secretary or receptionist. If you turn off the support staff members, there is a good chance they'll speak negatively about you to the boss.

It's a good idea to spend a little time preparing before the meeting. Make sure your resumé is up-to-date and print a few copies to bring with you. Read over your resumé the night before the meeting and think about what in your background might interest the person. Write a list of questions you would like to ask the person, but also think about what information about yourself you would like to share.

When you begin the meeting, give the person a firm handshake, look them in the eye and smile. Use their first name throughout the meeting, because people love hearing it. Right away, thank them for taking time to meet with you. Briefly explain, once again, why you are there and that you appreciate the opportunity to learn from their success.

At that point, it is okay to start your list of questions. As the person tells you about the industry and his or her career in particular, take some notes. This is flattering and shows that you are interested in what he or she is saying. Ask some unscripted follow-up questions based on what is said. This shows that you are a curious person and that you are truly listening.

The next thing you will do is extremely important. As you are asking your targeted person questions about his or her background, be sure to work in some information about yourself. If your targeted person says something that reminds you of an experience you've had, work that into the conversation. Overall, you should spend two thirds of the time asking your targeted person questions and one third telling information about yourself.

Toward the end of the meeting, pull out a copy of your resumé and hand it to your target. "Here's a current copy of my resumé," you say. "If you ever become aware of a career opportunity for which I would be suited, please feel free to forward my resumé. Of course, my contact information is on the resumé if you ever want to discuss any opportunity with me directly."

Nobody, absolutely nobody, hires someone they don't like.

Next, it's a good idea to say something like this: "You have been extremely helpful for me. I greatly appreciate it. Who else do you know in this industry who might be willing to speak with me and provide me with valuable information like you have?" This is a non-threatening way to get more contacts out of the person. Of course, you would follow up with any contact that a targeted person gives you.

Sincerely thank the person as you are leaving. Take an extra moment, look them in the eye, give them another smile and a firm handshake, and be on your way. As soon as you return to your computer, draft a thank you note and mail it immediately.

One of your key goals is to find common ground with the influential person you meet. You want to build rapport and get the person to like you. Chances are you are engaging in formal networking in hopes of getting a new job. If so, getting the person to like you is all important. Nobody, absolutely nobody, hires someone they don't like. Let's face it: You spend more time with your colleagues than you do with your family and friends. Therefore, you might as well work with someone you like.

THE OUTCOMES

A few conclusions could come from your meeting. At the very worst, no opportunity comes from the meeting, but you still have made a contact and learned about a new company/person/industry, while practicing your interviewing skills. Perhaps you impressed the targeted decision-maker, and he or she keeps you in mind. The next day, this person could be talking to a buddy at a Rotary meeting, who is looking to hire someone like you. You hope the person with whom you met would recommend you. Even better, your targeted person may have been so impressed with you that he or she finds a way to create a job specially designed just for you. Although this last possibility is the least likely, it is not far-fetched.

The more of these meetings you hold, the more likely something great will happen. We never know exactly when opportunity will show its face. Your goal should be to do all you can to facilitate as many opportunities as possible.

If you are going to use formal networking as a way to find your next great career opportunity, you should start now. Even if you are happy with your current job, start now. Formal networking is usually a slow method of job searching. It's highly effective, because you get the job just right for you. It's slow, however, because you normally have to meet with a number of people before the perfect fit becomes apparent to you and the future boss.

If you have big career ambitions, you can't afford to wait. The business world moves fast, so you have to be proactive not only to get ahead, but also to simply keep up. Don't waste time. Get started with formal networking now, so you can reap the rewards down the road.

CHAPTER EIGHT

Hand-to-Hand Combat: In the Trenches of Informal Networking

N OTHING IS MORE FUNDAMENTALLY PART OF SELF MARKETING THAN INFOR-
mal networking. It is the grassroots of self marketing. It is the actual hand-to-hand combat that goes on in the trenches of the business
world. You can strategize about using the media, you can build your own
website, and you can craft brilliant speeches, but ultimately nothing is
more effective than showing up at a party and pressing the flesh.

Informal networking is the nitty-gritty of self marketing. Informal
networking involves a lot of talking and schmoozing. It happens at
receptions, dinner parties, mixers, neighborhood association meetings
and during the breaks at an educational seminar. Any time you have
the chance to establish a positive relationship, you are engaging in at
least a basic level of networking. No matter how sophisticated your
marketing efforts may become using other channels, you still have to
be out in public meeting people, sharing information with them, asking them questions and memorizing their names.

Despite co-hosting a popular radio show and writing a regular newspaper column, I derive more self marketing benefits from just showing up at a chamber of commerce event, where I spend time chatting with other professionals.

I call it "informal," but effective networking is very purposeful and requires practice and planning. Networking is hard work especially if you are an introverted person. Even for extroverts, it requires a concerted effort in order for it to be successful. Having a goal makes informal networking much more effective. You're not just doing this for fun. If so, you would be better off taking a vacation to Disneyland instead.

Think about this term: *goal-based networking*. Your informal networking efforts should only *appear* to be informal. In reality they are planned and executed based on your desired outcomes. Goal-based networking means that you go to a social function with a purpose much deeper than eating free food and drinking someone else's booze. It means you work the crowd instead of huddling up in the corner with the co-workers who accompanied you.

In goal-based networking, you strive to accomplish the following:

- Get people to remember you;
- Get people to like you;
- Get people to know you;
- Get people to understand you; and
- Get people to refer business to you or give you some opportunity.

When you go to a business, political or social function, you should go into it thinking you will meet multiple people, some of whom will turn into clients or friends.

PERSONAL TARGET AUDIENCE

As we established in chapter two, self marketers have personal target audiences. These are the people to whom their self-marketing messages are directed. Your informal networking efforts should focus on your group of targeted influential people. It doesn't make much sense to go to an event populated entirely by people outside your target audience. You might end up having fun, but you won't advance your career.

As an early step in the goal-based networking process, make sure you understand exactly who your personal target audience is. It may be helpful to make a list of the types of people and the types of positions they hold. Next, make a list of the events and the places where you would have a high likelihood of interacting with members or your target audience.

For most professionals, target audience members can be found at chamber of commerce events, political functions, service clubs, fraternal organizations, philanthropic events, professional association meetings and conventions. Generally, your target audience consists of people who have the power, money or influence to do something beneficial for you. Once you have figured out where your targets are, you need to get involved in those organizations and show up at their events.

DON'T BE TOO EXCLUSIVE

One note of caution: Although you should spend the majority of your time networking with your target audience, don't fall into the elitism trap. Keep in mind that even the most unlikely of people you meet could lead to opportunities.

We've all heard stories of the multi-millionaire walking into a luxury car dealership wearing a ball cap and grubby clothes. The salespeople assume the person has no business being there and don't give him the time of day. That's a mistake. An average person could become quite successful at a later date. A "low-ranking" employee in some company could end up giving you a tip or recommending you to the higher-ups in his company. Some of the best real estate tips I've received over the years have come from people who never invested a penny in commercial real estate. Don't disrespect someone just because he or she is wearing grubby clothes and a ball cap and doesn't appear to be a member of your target audience.

I have given numerous speeches on career success and job searching to thousands of college students. When I talk to the students about informal networking, I always ask them to do a quick exercise. I tell them, "Please take a moment and look at the person sitting on your left." Next I say, "Now turn your head and look at the person sitting on your right. Remember those people, because there is a chance that one of them could be your boss some day." The students always laugh at this, especially when I say, "So you better start kissing up to them now."

The moral of the story is that you never know how someone you currently take for granted could benefit you at some point in the future. Another lesson that students derive from this little exercise is that it is never too early to start networking. Too often, college students assume that networking is something they do after they enter the "real world." That's short-sighted. If I had to do college all over again, I would spend more time developing relationships with more people, especially those who showed the signs of future greatness. If you can cement relationships early in your life, they will likely be more fruitful for you later in life.

MECHANICS OF INFORMAL NETWORKING

One of the first things you must accept about informal networking is that it requires a lot of small talk or chit-chat. Some people are a little inexperienced in the art of small talk, while others hate it or are even terrified by it. If you are not a natural conversationalist, I recommend you spend time practicing. This could involve standing in front of a mirror pretending to talk to another professional, or you could practice with a friend or family member. Another great way to practice is by going to non-intimidating networking events and practice on people you are more comfortable being around.

As you network with other professionals, focus on remembering names. Hearing someone utter my first name is very appealing to me as it is to almost everyone. If you use a person's first name, he or she instantly has a more positive opinion of you. Make sure that during a five-minute conversation with someone, you find a way to use his or her first name several times. Make a habit of this, and I guarantee it will pay off for you.

If you are the host or hostess of a networking event, please do everyone a favor and make nametags available. Some guests might grumble a bit about wearing a nametag, but they are truly helpful. Like a glass of good bourbon, nametags are a social lubricant at professional functions.

What separates great networkers from average ones is the ability to remember a person's name after you have met them. It is worth your while to concentrate on a person's name when you are introduced. Commit it to memory. Unfortunately, this is not easy for most people. For some reason, I occasionally forget a name just a couple minutes after meeting a person, even during the conversation! This is frustrating and potentially embarrassing. Some people are just naturally gifted with name-recollection skills. It's a common skill among politicians. I have heard stories of the first President Bush remembering the name of a person he had met months earlier. How flattering it is when a busy, powerful person remembers you long after you first met.

If you struggle to remember names, try making a little game out of it. When someone tells you her name, focus on her face and burn it into your memory. Next, try to think of something about her that reminds you of something else. This is called word association. In your mind, repeat her name and the associated idea over and over. Theoretically, you will think of her name and the associated word the next time you run into her.

Make a positive impression during initial introductions. This is important because other people make judgments about us in the first few seconds they meet us. That's why the very beginning of any encounter with another person is the most important. How do you do this? For one thing, be positive and enthusiastic. Most people prefer to be around energetic people, not negative, pessimistic mopes. When you meet someone, give them a firm handshake, smile and look them in the eye. Don't just *say*, "Pleased to meet you." Sincerely mean it.

As you begin an interpersonal interaction during a networking encounter, you should immediately be looking for some common ground between the other person and you. Finding something in common with your fellow conversationalist makes the situation much more comfortable. It does not matter who the person is or where you are, you can always find common ground with someone.

I was once in line for a ride at Disney World and started talking to the person next to me. Despite the fact that we were total strangers, both hundreds of miles from our respective homes, it only took a couple minutes to discover that we had a mutual acquaintance. As the old saying goes, the world is a small place. It is amazing how few layers you have to go through before you and a complete stranger can find a person you both know.

When you and your fellow conversationalist both know the same person, you have established one of the best forms of common ground.

While other people are a great focus for common-ground seekers, they are not the only thing you can have in common with someone. More typically, you can find common ground with someone by discussing a mutual interest. Whatever your hobby is, or whatever you do for a living, there's a good chance someone else at a networking function shares your interest. You just have to find out what it is. When you do, your conversation will not only flow more smoothly, it will be more rewarding and productive.

So, how do you find common ground? The best way is to ask questions, lots of questions. In a networking situation, question-asking is tremendously effective. Not only does questioning pull important information out of other people, it helps you build rapport and impress them. Questioning is very flattering. If you ask a person a question about himself or herself and appear to have a sincere interest, you will go a long way toward getting the person to like you. Most of us love it when others ask us questions. It's gratifying. It makes us feel important. It allows us to talk about our favorite subjects: ourselves.

In addition to being flattering, asking questions shows that you are strong, intelligent, curious and that you have leadership skills. Whoever is asking questions is actually in control of the conversation. By questioning, you set the agenda of the conversation. That's why successful, powerful people almost always ask a lot of questions.

If you're a smart networker, you will spend about two-thirds of the time talking about the other person, your fellow conversationalist, and his or her interests. Of the remaining one-third, half of it will be spent talking about other people/issues/ideas, and then, finally, the other half (or about one-sixth of the time) you will spend talking about you and your interests. This is hard to do, because nothing is more interesting to you than you and your interests. Do not focus on yourself.

Sometimes a hard-working networker will try so hard to ask questions and remember to discuss the other person's interests that he will forget to mention anything at all about himself. This is a mistake, because if you don't let the other person know at least something about you, you have missed an important self marketing opportunity.

There's another reason you don't want to go overboard on question asking. If you do nothing but ask questions, the other person will start to feel as if he's being interrogated. Nobody likes that feeling. Balance your questions and discussion of the other person's interests with something about yourself. When you do talk about yourself or your interests, be sure to choose something that will intrigue the other person.

The more you know about informal networking and the better you become in interpersonal situations, the more frustrated you might become with the ineptitude of others. My father is particularly gifted in the art of good conversation. He truly focuses on the other person, shows genuine interest in that person and asks great questions. He remembers first names and uses them regularly. Not only does he ask questions, but the next time he runs into the person, he actually remembers the answers.

This skill has been very useful for my dad, because everyone who meets him likes him. I can remember him telling me as a kid that I needed to ask questions and put the other person's interests ahead of my own. Sure enough, it works, but sometimes a person who is highly advanced in the art of interpersonal etiquette can get a little frustrated when others do not return the favor. On occasion, my dad has expressed surprise that few people will show similar interpersonal attention back to him. I have noticed the same thing. Of course, those who do return the favor make a positive impression on me.

It's tempting to get mad when someone does not reciprocate your interpersonal diligence, but that's a mistake. It's best to be very forgiving of others' interpersonal flaws. Most people are either unskilled or so narcissistic that they simply have no desire to ask me anything about myself. If this happens to you, just brush it off and forget about it. Keep exercising good interpersonal skills, and you will get ahead in life. The fact that so many people are so damned self-centered is actually a benefit to self marketers who know what they're doing. A good self marketer knows how to take advantage of a self-absorbed person.

> **It's best to be very forgiving of others' interpersonal flaws.**

There is a reason why you are networking with the self-absorbed person. It's self marketing pure and simple. You have a goal for your relationship with that person. Ultimately, you want to get that person to like and respect you and have positive feelings toward you with the hope that it will lead to some desired opportunity. The more narcissistic a person is, the easier he is to manipulate.

It is important to give something of value when you are in a networking encounter. A good networker knows that conversation is more than just exchanging pleasantries. To truly get a person to buy into all that you are, you must give him something of value. By "value," I do not mean something tangible. I'm talking about information, insight, humor or a fascinating piece of trivia.

So, in addition to the interpersonal techniques discussed here, you also have to have a verbal give-away. As I've mentioned before, I work in commercial real estate and I co-host *Grow Omaha*, a radio show on economic development. Therefore, I know a great deal about construction projects, businesses expanding in my city and retailers moving to town. When I'm networking with fellow Omaha residents, the pieces of value I give out usually have something to do with local economic growth and development. I'm also a fairly humorous guy, so I'll often use humor as my valuable give-away.

I have a business acquaintance who sends me an email on the first of each month. Never does a month go by without that familiar email. Before you start thinking that this person is an amazingly diligent self marketer, you should know this: It's always the SAME email. It never changes, which leads me to believe it's programmed into some contact-management software. Here's what it says: "Hey, how are things going with you?" Instead of being an effective form of interpersonal communication, it is annoying. It shows no creativity. It is not at all personalized to me. It gives me nothing. I feel as if that kind of "networking" is all take-take-take. He obviously wants me to think about him so he emails me regularly. However, he doesn't want to go to any effort to engage me and interest me; he simply wants to cross off the monthly obligation of touching base with Jeff Beals. Avoid sending worthless messages like "we should get together sometime," when you have no intention of ever getting together.

Whatever you decide to give away, find some piece of information that is both interesting and useful. The people with whom you network will be even more impressed with you and will think more positively about you. If people know they are always going to hear something worthwhile when they meet with you, they will go out of their way to talk to you. When that happens, you can smile and feel satisfaction that you are doing a great job as a networker and ultimately a self marketer.

One of the most common questions you will be asked in an informal networking encounter is, "What do you do?" Be prepared to answer this question clearly and concisely. Some people will beat around the bush with long-winded, jargon-laden answers about their job and their employer. Even worse, some people will drag out this meandering explanation of their vocation for several minutes. Listening to that is torture. Anytime someone does this to me, I feel like pouring gasoline all over myself and striking a match. Please, find a way to clearly explain your job and your company in less than 30 seconds using words that your average layman can understand.

Remember your ultimate goal in networking is to build rapport in hopes of getting something of value. Most of your time will be spent making others feel good, but at some point you need to cash in. Eventually, you're going to have to ask for the job, account, the information or whatever opportunity you desire from the relationship. In my company, we get a kick out of some of the "business development" representatives prospective vendors send our way. There's one guy in particular whom we find quite entertaining. He constantly comes by to give us gifts and take us to lunch. In aggregate, we have received hundreds of dollars worth of free stuff from this guy over the last several years.

What's interesting is that this business development guy has never once asked us for our business! Why is he wasting his time and money on us? We laugh about it and treat it like a game. How many times can we get him to buy us drinks/lunches/gifts before he tries to close a sale? Perhaps his strategy is to do so much for us that someday we feel sorry for him and volunteer to be his client. Another possibility is that he just networks for the sake of networking. In other words, he once heard, "Successful people must network." That's true, but it doesn't do much for you if you're not willing to ask for the order.

TRACKING AND CONTACTING

To maximize your informal networking efforts, one of your goals must be to organize and be able to recall information about the people you meet. As I said earlier in the chapter, don't let the name "informal networking" convince you that it is anything but a planned, calculated and organized endeavor. In fact, organization is a critical requirement in order for your networking to be considered goal-based.

When you meet someone new, get in the habit of offering your business card. Never go to a function without a healthy supply of business cards. I keep a stack of them in each of my suit jackets, in all of my coats, my wallet and my leather portfolio folder. As an added safety measure, I have business cards at home and in my car. That way, I am never without them. Business cards are a critical self marketing aid. They must always be ready. You never know when you will need one.

I often run into members of my personal target audience on the weekend while dressed in jeans and a sweatshirt. You never know when business calls, so be ready to answer at all times.

By the way, it's a good idea to offer someone a business card even if it is the second time you have met her. For all you know, she could have lost your card or forgotten your name. By automatically handing her your card, you make it easier for her. She doesn't have to feel socially ungraceful, apologizing for not remembering your name. Ultimately, a polished networker smiles, shakes hands, says hi and offers a business card in one fluid, comfortable motion.

If the other person doesn't offer you her business card when you first meet her, ask her for it. Put it in a shirt pocket, your purse or somewhere safe. As soon as you return to your office, enter the information into whatever database you use: your contact management software, your personal data assistant or your cell phone. I have about 1,000 names in my personal database list. My professional database has almost 5,000 email addresses. If you are serious about being a successful networker, you are consequently in the list management business. You must build a big, diverse group of professionals you can call on in a moment of need. Good list management techniques are necessary to maintain the list, organize it and keep your list current.

Once you have a decent list of contacts, don't waste any time putting it to use. Find excuses to make contacts with the people on your list. After all, one of the goals of networking is to reinforce your positive image and build name recognition in the minds of other people. You want to make other people like you. That's done through personal contact.

If you know someone's birthday, put it on your electronic calendar as a recurring event. That way, you'll be reminded automatically each year. When that reminder pops up, send the person a birthday greeting either via email or snail mail. The tiny amount of time you invest in such a kind gesture could return to you 10-fold.

If you run across an article that reminds you of a person, email it to them. Do whatever it takes; find an excuse to make contact with people in your database on a periodic basis. Just make sure the contact is something more valuable than a "Hi! Hope you're doing well!"

I write a regular column for a local newspaper. I am also interviewed periodically for stories in my area of expertise. It seems like every time one of my articles runs, I get positive, unsolicited feedback. Sometimes, one of my acquaintances will cut a clipping and send it to me. Other times, I might get an email from someone I've never met, telling me the article appealed to him. I have to admit that I love such feedback. It motivates me to keep going. Given that, I naturally have very positive feelings for anyone who takes the time to compliment my hard work. If you do the same thing, people will be touched, and they'll remember your kind gesture for a long time.

DEALING WITH SOCIAL DISCOMFORT

For many people, networking is a painful experience. If you are shy, you have to find a way to break out of it and muster the courage to speak to total strangers. It's a simple fact: Networking is intimidating for a significant portion of the population.

If you fall into that category, don't feel as if you're alone. I'm a very active networker, but I've had to work at it. I'm not someone who was blessed naturally with a great deal of social competence. I've had to hone my craft over many years. To this day, I sometimes get tinges of uneasiness when I walk up to a building where some high-powered cocktail reception is being held.

You can deal with shyness in a number of ways. First of all, I believe in practice. There is absolutely nothing wrong with rehearsing how you will act in a networking encounter the night before in the quiet privacy of your own home. It also helps to observe others. Think of someone you know who is socially gifted, very at ease working a room. Watch that person. Study that person. Think how you can imitate him. Each time you go to a networking event, try to do something he does. The best ideas are borrowed. Instead of reinventing the wheel, figure out how you can mimic someone who has already figured it out.

I don't want to sound like I'm advocating alcohol, but holding a drink at a social function helps you be more comfortable. If you're a non-drinker, there is nothing wrong with holding a soda or virgin cocktail. The drink is useful, because it gives you something to do with your hands. It also gives you the opportunity to look down at it every once in awhile. That's handy, because sometimes it gets hard to constantly stare into someone's eyes.

For better or worse, drinking is a prominent part of socialization in our culture. You just have to be careful not to become intoxicated. You don't want to do anything that would embarrass you or damage the reputation you are working so hard to build. Some networkers will order one drink and nurse it for a couple hours, just taking tiny sips infrequently. I know of one person who orders a 7-Up with just a tiny amount of alcohol in it. That way, it smells like a drink, but there's not enough live juice in it to compromise his faculties.

Another way of dealing with shyness is to envision success before going to an event. Like a coach mentally preparing athletes for a big game, you can increase your likelihood for success by imagining yourself doing very well in a social situation. Sit down for a few minutes in the quiet of your home or behind your closed office door and envision yourself saying the right things, using good interpersonal skills and being professionally assertive. If you do this regularly, you will most likely evolve into a savvy networker.

Fear can lead to shyness. Perhaps you are afraid you'll look stupid. Perhaps you're afraid to interrupt someone at a party. Most significantly, the fear could be that you will be rejected. Even as an adult, it is a very unpleasant experience to introduce yourself and attempt to carry on a conversation with someone who clearly appears not to give a damn about you. I know – it's happened to me plenty of times! When it happens to you, just brush it off and go to the next person. You can only control your behavior and emotions. When someone gives you a cold shoulder, it likely means that person's problems are greater than yours.

Shyness can also be caused by feelings of personal inadequacy you might have. Please don't let that stop you. For one thing, everyone on earth has at least some inadequacies; nobody is perfect. Successful people are the ones who accomplish things in spite of their inadequacies. Also, just because you think you are inadequate in one area doesn't mean that other people will pick up on it.

My experience has convinced me the opposite is true. Quite frankly, most people perceive us to be greater than we actually are. I call it the-grass-is-always-greener-on-the-other-side syndrome. It's easy to assume that other people have better lives, are more organized and are living life more richly. You should realize that other people are thinking that about YOU. Some people are envious of you and perceive you to be much more accomplished than you really are. So, if you ever get that feeling of inadequacy, and it tempts you to stay home rather than go network at some important event, just tell yourself that other people assume you are much stronger and confident than you really are.

> Quite frankly, most people perceive us to be greater than we actually are. I call it the-grass-is-always-greener-on-the-other-side syndrome.

If you do enough networking, you start to feel a natural rhythm or flow. Good networkers flow from one person to the next. They make positive impressions. They help people feel good about themselves. A gifted networker appears to transition effortlessly from one interpersonal situation to another. He'll start speaking to one person, but before he leaves the conversation, he introduces someone else, essentially finding his replacement. He then seems to transcend the crowd as he transitions to the next person.

You may wonder how long you should talk to one person during a networking encounter. There is no universal answer. You have to read each situation individually. At a party or reception, two people will introduce themselves, ask a couple mostly superficial questions of each other and then meld into other interpersonal situations. You don't want to monopolize someone else's time, nor do you want to waste all of your time on one person. That said, there will be periodic situations where you and another networker will hit it off and discover a bunch of mutual interests. If it feels right, keep on talking. You have to go with your gut instinct.

Periodically, I'll be at a party, reception or some other networking event, and I'll suddenly find myself standing alone with nobody to talk to. This can be a little unnerving. Whenever this happens, I get the instant thought: "Oh, no, people will think I'm an anti-social loser!" For a moment, it's almost like going back to the awkward days of adolescence. When this happens, don't panic. Just look around for another person standing by herself, go up to her and introduce yourself.

If there are no other "single" people, it is perfectly acceptable to go up to a twosome or threesome. This can be intimidating, because you feel as if you're interrupting. Don't worry about it. Just go up to the couple or group and blend in. Sometimes it helps to say, "Mind if I join you?"

Now, when you are already talking to someone else and a third person comes up to you, be sure to include that person and make them feel welcome. Treat the conversational newcomer the same way you would like to be treated. Don't act as if you're inconvenienced. Just introduce yourselves and allow the person to feel part of the group. The tone of your voice and your body language will help make such a person feel more welcome. For instance, when a third person comes up me when I'm already talking to someone, I slightly turn my body toward the new person. This makes the person feel subconsciously included and welcome. I always smile and speak positively. If the person comes in mid-conversation, I explain what we've been talking about in an effort to bring the new person up to speed.

Just remember how it feels to be that outside person. If you're welcoming, people will like you, and that is one of your primary purposes for networking.

While preparing to go to some function, have you ever worried, "What if I don't know anyone there?" It's a common concern, but knowing nobody at a networking event is actually a blessing if you have the right attitude. When nobody knows you, you are liberated from all preconceived notions. You have a clean slate. You can establish your image any way you want in front of these new people.

Not knowing anyone also forces you to reach out and actually use your networking skills. Too many people will go to a function and sit in the corner with their friends, co-workers, spouse, whoever. That's a waste of time and money. If you're going to do that, just go to a restaurant.

I usually drive by myself to a networking function. I find that I meet more people this way and get more out of the event. You just have to set aside your shyness, your self-doubts and any personal inadequacies you may be harboring. Just get inside, go up to people and introduce yourself. Once you get used to showing up at events by yourself, you may just realize you prefer it that way. Another advantage of driving by yourself to the function is that you can leave whenever you like.

MORE ART THAN SCIENCE

Ultimately, good networking is an art, a craft that needs to be developed constantly and practiced regularly. Networking success also depends on creativity and diversity. You can't go to the same functions that draw the same people and expect to meet fresh faces. You can't keep doing the same type of networking over and over again and expect to get new results.

Networking requires energy and commitment. There will be times when you're tired and not feeling very well. Nevertheless, you must dig deep and find the strength to get through it. If you can't put on a good show, don't step in front of the audience.

Networking is perpetual. You can't go out and network heavily for a few months and then expect people to remember you for a lifetime. Keep in mind that networking is a form of self marketing. In any marketing endeavor, the principles of repetition and frequency are of paramount importance. That means your networking efforts do not end until you put yourself out to pasture.

Harness the Media

EVERY MORNING I OPEN MY EMAIL ACCOUNT, AND I'M INUNDATED WITH messages from publicists representing authors and expert speakers. They implore me to book their clients on *Grow Omaha*, my weekly radio show. Some of these talent agents will also send snail-mail solicitations and call me at the office.

I book less than 10 percent of these guest experts, because most of the interview subjects don't fit my show's narrowly focused format. Nevertheless, the persistent publicists keep pitching the same people over and over. There's a reason why they are so persistent: They have a lot at stake. Nothing is more powerful in promoting a person, a company or a brand than free news coverage, also known as "earned media."

It is much more effective to have a story written about you in a newspaper or to be interviewed on a radio or television show than it is to purchase an advertisement. Consumers are suspicious of advertising. They know ads are purchased and therefore biased in favor of whoever purchased them. If your publicity appears to be part of a normal story or talk show, you are much more believable. People trust the accuracy and authenticity of the message. People don't feel as if they're being sold something.

Harnessing the media might be the most efficient way to self market. You get the most bang for the buck – for a relatively small amount of work, your message and your name are carried to a large group of media. Journalism is referred to as "mass communication," because you are blasting your message simultaneously to a huge group of people.

Think about this way: If you network one-on-one with a person over lunch, you spend one hour making an impression on one person. If you write an article in a community magazine, you could spend four or five hours writing to make an impression on thousands of people. If you were able to score a quote in the *Wall Street Journal*, you would be spending a few minutes of interview time in order to reach millions of readers. Mass media isn't the most intimate form of self marketing, but it is hands down the most efficient.

Anyone who controls the media has great power.

Every professional in the world needs to become a recognized expert in something and then market himself or herself to the personal target audience. If expert speakers and authors work hard to earn publicity in the media, shouldn't you? Of course! You may not be the type of expert who goes on a 10-city promotional tour, but you need to market your expertise at least within your industry or your local market. To do that, you can harness the power of the media.

The media are very powerful. Our society is obsessed with media. Most of us consume large amounts of it each day. Whether it is printed, broadcasted, or Internet-based, and regardless of whether it is informational or entertaining, the media are extremely important to us. The media shape public opinion and motivate consumers to buy. They start trends and play a major role in defining our culture.

Anyone who controls the media has great power. That's why media companies and executives have so much influence. There have been many times when media outlets have been able to foist their will on the unsuspecting public. For instance, some media experts claim Walter Cronkite of CBS singlehandedly sparked America's opposition to the

Vietnam War by coming out against it on national television. Newspaper editorials have been directly responsible for the margin between victory and defeat for numerous political candidates. Small biases in media coverage can lead to the making or breaking of one's political career. As media mogul William Randolph Hearst once said, "You can crush a man with journalism."

I remember an interesting case study in my community. A local businessman decided to run for U.S. Senate. Campaigning as a Republican, he portrayed himself as a successful business owner and a devoted husband and father. He was a boastful guy, bragging about his business prowess and calling his house the "premier home in the city." Unfortunately for this would-be Senator, the local newspaper did an investigative story on him and discovered improprieties in his background. The article even divulged that this professed family man had a son from an earlier relationship. The son didn't even know him and didn't receive any money from him. The candidate's political career was instantly ruined.

Make no doubt about it – the media are a tremendous force in our society. As you work to harness the media, always remember to be respectful of them. As with any powerful tool, if you use it wisely, it is effective. If you use it improperly, media can kill you.

All together, the media comprise one of the most powerful institutions in the world, but that doesn't mean that individuals can't harness the media and use some of that power to benefit themselves. In fact, to be effective as a self marketer, you must find a way to manipulate the media to your favor.

CONTROL OF THE MEDIA

One way to harness the power of the media is to actually control part of it. This can be a difficult and expensive thing to do but highly effective if you can pull it off. You can gain control by buying a media company or starting your own media outlet. You might also buy a section of a newspaper or time on a broadcast station.

Many companies buy time on television and radio for infomercials. Essentially, the advertiser "owns" the medium during the time it leases from the station. If a company doesn't want to produce a cheesy infomercial, it may purchase the sponsoring rights to a respected and popular show. Although these are expensive ways to control the media, individual people can take advantage of them too.

If you can't afford to buy your own show or buy your own column in a newspaper, perhaps you could partner with other people, thus sharing the cost burden. It is common for real estate agents to band together to buy time on local television stations to showcase the houses they have listed. While these shows are rarely responsible for actually selling a house, they do wonders for the real estate agents who are trying to establish name recognition in the community.

To get the *Grow Omaha* radio show up and running, my company bought time on a local radio station. As the show gained popularity, we were recruited by a much bigger station. Although *Grow Omaha* now has an audience of almost 10,000 listeners per week, who consider the show to be one of the most authoritative sources of information on Omaha's economy, in the very beginning, it was just an unproven paid program.

By purchasing time on the radio station, we were effectively able to control the media. Now, just because you control time on the media doesn't mean listeners and viewers will pay any attention to you. We had to work hard to provide an outstanding product that kept listeners tuning in. We had to make the show of genuine use and interest to our audience and not an hour-long infomercial for Coldwell Banker Commercial World Group. Sure, we mentioned our company name, but we mostly focused on quality programming. If you ever decide to purchase a show, make sure you make it interesting first and of promotional benefit to you second.

If you can't afford to *buy* part of the media, you might be able to *create* your own niche. Newsletters are an innovative form of home-grown media. Based on your area of expertise, create a newsletter that contains articles and features that would interest your target audience. It's not easy to produce a worthwhile newsletter, and it takes effort to build a distribution list, but once you do, the rewards can be significant.

Before the *Grow Omaha* radio program existed, I was covering the same content in a quarterly newsletter. I wrote articles and provided interesting, entertaining tidbits about Omaha's growth and development to the types of people who would be interested in such a topic. Known as *The World Group Leader*, this newsletter has become very popular and now has an electronic circulation of 5,000 copies. Like the radio show, the newsletter is successful because its first priority is to provide useful information. Marketing our company is the second priority. Because of that, readers enjoy it. They don't feel as if they're reading a four-page commercial. If you choose to do a newsletter or if you decide to control any other form of media, make sure you deliver worthwhile content. If you do, you can proudly plaster your name and photo on it; the self-marketing component takes care of itself.

If you create your own media niche, don't stop with just one form of media. To maximize your self marketing benefit, integrate your message into multiple delivery mechanisms. In addition to the *Grow Omaha* show, I use my expertise in economic development to market myself by using a newsletter, the GrowOmaha.com website and accompanying discussion forum, a weekly e-blast to 5,000 members of my company's target audience. In addition to that, I write a bi-weekly column on economic development for a local newspaper, and I give 50 to 75 speeches each year on Omaha's growth and development to any group that will have me.

Controlling the media has collateral benefits that can further expand your reach. For instance, the *Grow Omaha* show allows us to use "trade out" to carry our message through additional media outlets. We struck a deal with Family Fun Center, a local indoor entertainment business that has a huge video display screen near the city's busiest intersection, which carries 100,000 cars per day. Family Fun Center gets ads on our radio show, while we get an announcement on their display screen.

As I've said before, I chose to make economic development my area of expertise because it interested me and related closely to my profession, commercial real estate. It doesn't matter what expertise area you choose. You just need to develop one and then package it in a message format that is interesting and lends itself to multiple forms of media. Be a bold visionary. You may have doubts as to whether the subject matter will be effective for your self marketing. Frankly, as long as you are interesting, the subject matter you choose isn't the most important thing.

MANIPULATING THE MEDIA

If you don't want to buy or create your own media niche, there are plenty of ways you can use media that already exist.

The first thing to remember in the media manipulation game is to be *useful*. Journalists are time-starved people who live under constant deadline pressure. Each and every day, they have to find a way to fill blank newspaper space or hours of air time. They tend to appreciate anyone who can help them fill the white space with quality material. If you can do this, journalists will use you regularly.

Successful self marketers make journalists' jobs easier. There is nothing wrong with developing personal friendships with journalists in your city or with those who cover your industry in national journals or trade magazines. If a reporter needs some information quickly, they are likely to pick up the phone and ask a trusted friend with the appropriate knowledge and experience.

You can develop a good relationship with journalists by supplying them the hard-to-find information. Sometimes you need to take the initiative. If I have a big story, as I often do in my area of expertise, I call the reporters with whom I have the best relationships. This strengthens our relationship, because every reporter wants to be the first to receive new information. It makes them look better in front of the boss. I have been doing this long enough that I often receive phone calls from journalists hunting for story ideas.

I am often quoted in the newspaper or interviewed on television. Any reporter who calls me gets accurate information from an expert in the field and ready-to-publish quotes. I'm always ready to supply reporters with an opinion, a different perspective and a useful quote. It behooves you to become a reliable source for news stories.

A good self marketer is always looking for excuses to be quoted in the paper or interviewed by radio and television. In your quest for media exposure, never do anything that embarrasses you or tarnishes your reputation. As long as you maintain your professional dignity, I encourage you to find ways to get in the news.

You should constantly think of what you are doing and if there is a news angle to it. Likewise, if something happens in your area of expertise, even if you personally have nothing to do with it, it's still an opportunity. Call media outlets and volunteer yourself as an expert source willing to comment on the news of the day.

Successful self marketers make journalists' jobs easier.

No matter how big an expert you become and no matter how close a relationship you build with the journalists, there is no guarantee that all of your material will make the news. Be very forgiving about this. It is up to the self marketer to keep pro-
viding information. If a journalist doesn't use something you provide, just let it go like water rolling off a duck's feathers. One of the quickest ways to ruin your relationship with journalists is to pressure them or try to slap a guilt trip on them for not using your ideas. A self marketer must be willing to be used and abused, so to speak. You are thrilled when you are used by the media, but sometimes they will abuse you (in the form of blowing you off, ignoring you and taking you for granted). For better or worse, that's just how the game is played.

You should always remember to be on your guard when talking to a journalist. Don't say anything you don't want reported. Assume there is no "off the record." Even if you befriend a journalist, her job is not to be your cheerleader or personal publicist. Journalists always want the news angle, and in most cases they usually are more attracted to the negative side of any story. As former President Lyndon B. Johnson once said, "If one morning I walked on top of the water across the Potomac River, the headline that afternoon would read: 'President Can't Swim.'"

If you have achieved a good deal of success in your career, or if there is a unique aspect about your career, encourage local media to do features on you. Industry magazines often do features on professionals who have compelling stories or who have accomplished something special. Local newspapers and tabloids often feature individuals in the community.

Maintain an up-to-date database of media contact information. Your database should be divided by media type – newspaper, magazine, radio, television, Internet. To develop your list, it is perfectly acceptable to call the media company and ask which reporter is responsible for covering your area of expertise. Get to know the reporters and editors on your database and keep their information current.

If you are having a hard time getting quoted in the newspaper or convincing a magazine to do a feature article on you, you can take matters into your own hands. Most print publications accept letters to the editor. These allow you to express an interesting opinion and get your name printed and delivered to thousands of people. A more in-depth version of a letter to the editor is an "op-ed" piece, otherwise known as a guest editorial.

Unless you are already a rock star in your community or profession, it's difficult to get an op-ed piece published. Don't let that stop you. If you have truly developed an area of expertise, and you can communicate that expertise in an interesting format to a mass audience, go ahead and write an op-ed. If a major newspaper prints it, you will receive massive exposure, boosting your name recognition and doing wonders for your positive reputation. If there is anything controversial in your op-ed piece, you may end up receiving additional name exposure in the following couple of days; readers may be motivated to write letters to the editor agreeing with or disputing your op-ed. Most of these letters will probably make mention of your name.

PRESS RELEASES

Although not as effective as building personal relationships with reporters, press releases are efficient, low-cost and non-intrusive ways of delivering your information to media organizations. Companies use press releases all the time to announce new products or staff members. Newspapers are always looking for bits of information to fill little holes here and there throughout the paper. When looking to fill holes, editors will commonly go through their stack (or electronic files) of press releases looking to find something newsworthy.

Anytime you get a new job or promotion, encourage your employer to send a press release to your national industry publications as well as to your local newspapers. Always make sure your headshot photo is attached. You will be amazed how often your information will be printed. If you are self-employed, you have free reign to send out as many press releases as you would like. Just make sure the content of the releases is newsworthy and follows the generally accepted norms of press-release writing.

You should write your press releases using Associated Press style. Most journalistic publications use AP style in their writing. Press releases already written in AP style require less work on the editor's part. To learn AP style, you can pick up the official stylebook in the reference section at any of the major bookstores.

Just like newspaper articles, press releases should follow the "inverted pyramid" method of writing. Picture an upside-down pyramid. The fat base of the pyramid is at the top, and it represents the biggest, most significant, most newsworthy part of the story. The small, narrow tip of the pyramid is at the bottom. It represents the least meaningful part of the story.

Inverted-pyramid writing places great emphasis on the first sentence, referred to as the "lead." A good newspaper reporter conveys a great deal of information in that one opening sentence. He puts that short sentence at the very beginning of his article. You should do the same thing with your press releases. Before writing your first press release, sit down with a copy of the newspaper. Notice how reporters write leads. Copy that style in your own writing.

One of the advantages of the inverted-pyramid style is that editors can cut off the story at any point, but the most meaningful message remains.

Press release headlines should also incorporate the tenets of good journalism. Although some newspapers blatantly violate these rules, headlines are supposed to be present tense and use only action verbs. You should avoid conjugations of the verb "to be" such as "is" and "are." Like lead sentences, headlines should convey the press release's primary message in a succinct manner.

Most of your writing should be in active voice instead of passive voice. Examples of active-voice writing are these: "Susan moved to a new cubicle" and "President Bush vetoed the bill." Examples of passive-voice writing include these reverse examples: "The move was made by Susan" and "The bill was vetoed by President Bush."

The active voice is just clearer and easier to read. Likewise, all press releases should use straight-forward, unambiguous and generally simple sentences. There's an old saying that newspaper articles are written to someone with an eighth-grade education, meaning they are not terribly complex or intellectual in nature. Press releases should follow the same philosophy.

Use proper grammar. Proofread your press release carefully. Make sure your word tenses are consistent and that your subjects and verbs agree. Nothing is more unimpressive to a journalist than a press release full of syntax errors, typos and ambiguous messages.

Like newspaper articles, press releases should be short. Less is more! When I write press releases, I try to keep them to one page, including the header and any contact information.

Your press release should include several elements in addition to the body copy and headline. It should include a date or time when the content can be considered public knowledge. Many releases state "FOR IMMEDIATE RELEASE" near the top of the page. If you do not intend your release to be public right away, you can write, "EMBARGOED UNTIL (DATE & TIME)."

Press releases should include a contact person's name, telephone number and email address. Your full address and website should be listed at the bottom. Toward the end of the body copy, most press release writers have some "boilerplate" language. This is usually a final paragraph that stays the same in each press release.

If I was writing a press release about myself, my boilerplate language might read, "Jeff Beals is vice president of operations of Coldwell Banker Commercial World Group, a commercial real estate company serving Nebraska and western Iowa. He is co-host of *Grow Omaha*, a weekly economic development talk show on News Radio 1110 KFAB. Additionally, he serves as a part-time professor and freelance writer."

If your press release goes on to a second page, type "(more)" at the bottom of the first page. At the very end of the press release, type "#." This signifies to the newspaper editor that no more copy remains.

It is important to know to whom you are sending your press release. If your press release is directly related to the accounting profession, it does not make much sense if you send it to an architecture magazine. While it is still okay to mail hard copies of press releases to news organizations, I have had more success when I send electronic copies. This allows the editor to copy and paste your material into the publication without going to a lot of trouble. If you email a press release that pertains to you, attach a headshot photo of yourself.

If you become a serious press release writer, you may want to join PR Newswire or a similar press release distribution service. PR Newswire provides distribution services on behalf of thousands of clients worldwide. It sends press releases to news outlets in 135 countries and 40 languages. Becoming a member isn't cheap, but it's useful for certain people and organizations. For news consumers, press release services are handy sources of ideas and information.

PROFESSIONALISM

When dealing with the media, it is critical that you maintain a professional image at all times. If your professionalism is compromised, you could come across badly on television. You could also alienate a reporter, thus hurting your chances for more interviews later.

You must be interesting and relevant. Flashing some on-camera charisma helps too, but being interesting is even more important. Just as important is accuracy. Never embarrass the reporter (and yourself) by passing off rumors as fact. That will fatally damage your relationship with the reporter and ultimately could make you look stupid in front of your target audience.

Whether you are being interviewed by print or broadcast media, avoid using industry jargon. Nobody outside your field of expertise understands it. By using it, you are distancing yourself from the audience. Likewise, don't try to impress people by using an inordinate number of million-dollar words. Most people can see through this, which makes you look like an egotistical show-off. A highly developed vocabulary is a good thing, but not if you are using it merely to look more important.

Clichés are okay as long as they are not overdone. Also be careful not to fall into a trap that catches a lot of men in particular – using way too many sports clichés to describe business actions. It drives me nuts every time I hear "step up to the plate" and "we hit a home run."

Deliberately avoid using politically correct language. Most journalists like to convey their messages in straight-forward, unambiguous English. You should too. People roll their eyes when they hear obnoxious double speak. Don't say "career alternative enhancement program" when you mean "layoffs." Don't say "television with non-multi-color capability" when you mean "black-and-white." It's just painful to listen to or read such crap. There is a camping equipment dealer in my community that advertises on local radio stations. They actually have the gall to describe used RVs as "pre-enjoyed." Politically correct, double-speak language turns people off and can backfire on you. When answering interview questions, don't waste the reporter's time with a bunch of gibberish. Get to the point.

You can be a little more verbose in print-media interviews, but don't overdo it. The broadcast medium is a different animal. When you are interviewed by radio and television reporters, you need to speak in "sound bites." Your answers should be meaty and interesting but only about 20 seconds in length. Remember that broadcasting is a fast-moving media. Broadcasters take just the most interesting, short segments of interviews (known as sound bites) and replay them as part of stories or "packages" on the news. Many of these packages are only a minute or two in length. If you want your voice to be placed in a news story, you must learn to speak in sound bites.

Politicians are the masters of sound-bite speaking. They always speak in a series of sound bites so any part of their speech would fit nicely into the evening news. A Senator's speech, delivered on the floor of Congress, is designed so that any 20-second part of it could be pulled for a news clip. If you want to self market in the broadcast media, start practicing sound-bite speaking now.

Politically correct, double-speak language turns people off and can backfire on you.

Portraying the right image in the media is so important that many executives, entrepreneurs and politicians hire media coaches. These people are trained in the ways of journalism and often worked in media earlier in their careers. Using these professionals can truly improve your image especially if you are inexperienced with the media. They can also be quite helpful if you feel shy or awkward around reporters. Media coaches can teach you the right way to answer questions as well as when and how to avoid answering a question. They can even advise you on what clothing to wear during a television interview. As an additional service, some media coaches also help their clients with public speaking.

There are some negative aspects to hiring a media coach. The more established coaches can be quite expensive, plus those coaches who don't know what they're doing could make you so focused on perfect fundamentals that you end up portraying yourself as robotic and rehearsed instead of genuine and authentic.

Speak and Write Your Way Out of Obscurity

S EVERAL MONTHS AFTER I BEGAN A SIDE JOB WRITING ARTICLES FOR THE *Midlands Business Journal*, I ran into MBJ's editor at a real estate conference. We chatted for awhile and then she asked me, "Do you enjoy writing for us?" I assured her that I did.

Then she asked if it was helping my career. I got the sense she was fishing for something. Since her paper paid me only fifty bucks a story, she knew I wasn't doing it for the money. I told her it had been extremely beneficial to my career in many ways: In researching stories, I learned about other businesses. Each byline boosted my name recognition. It was a great opportunity to practice writing, and most importantly, I met influential people.

The editor nodded her head, seemingly happy to hear my response, saying, "I just don't understand why more business people like you don't write for us." She was frustrated, because local newspapers are always searching for writers.

I thought about what she said and wondered why more self marketers don't take advantage of writing opportunities. Working on those business articles was great for me. It was really the first way I established my name in the mass media and started to become well known in my community. Working with my sources, however, was an even more valuable part of the experience.

One of the first MBJ articles assigned to me was a feature on Mortgage Alliance, a mortgage brokerage company. My source was Pete Coen, who ran the office. I enjoyed interviewing Pete, so I kept in touch with him. In the years since then, we have developed a lasting friendship and a mutually beneficial business relationship. He handled my loan when I bought a new house in 2004. He also volunteers to speak about mortgage brokering each semester to my students at the University of Nebraska. My real estate company had the privilege of representing Mortgage Alliance when Pete wanted new office space. All of this started because I interviewed him for a newspaper article.

In many cases my presence in the print media has led directly to a new business opportunity. A woman once called our real estate office to list a former florist shop for lease in a trendy urban neighborhood. She talked with one of our agents who asked her how she heard about us. She responded, "I read Jeff Beals's columns in *The City Weekly*, so I thought I'd call you guys." We ended up leasing that space and collecting a commission a few weeks later.

Over the past few years, I have written more than 200 articles that have been published in about a dozen periodicals, some national and some local. On numerous occasions, someone who has read one of the articles wants to meet with me to discuss real estate. Often these meetings lead to a real estate deal for our company.

Giving speeches is similar to writing in that a relatively small amount of time and effort leads to an opportunity to make a positive impression in front of a number of people. Several years ago, I decided to become an active public speaker. I now give between 50 and 75 speeches a year. Locally, most of my presentations address economic growth and development, the topic I cover on my radio show. I also regularly travel out of town, speaking to college students about career success and job-searching techniques.

It is truly amazing the personal and business opportunities that have come my way from giving so many speeches. Speaking is one of the primary ways to establish your expertise in a certain area. It gives you great credibility and bolsters your name recognition. After every speech I give, audience members come up to me, asking for a business card. I frequently receive calls the day after a speech from listeners requesting a one-on-one meeting with me. These meetings sometimes lead to business opportunities. At the very least, they always yield some valuable information and a new friendship. I simply cannot say enough about the tremendous advantages that come from speaking and writing. They are effective, low-cost and very reasonable ways of getting your name known.

BECOMING LIKE THE MEDIA

In the previous chapter, we discussed how to harness the media. Now that you know how to do that, perhaps you should consider becoming part of the media. Writing articles and giving speeches are ideal ways of becoming part of the media machine in order to market yourself to large groups of people.

Speaking allows you to go over the heads of the media. As a speaker, you only need to convince a group to invite you. That can be a lot easier than getting a media outlet to run a positive article or broadcast feature on you.

Writing and speaking also allow you to replicate your message over and over, 24 hours a day. As a published writer and active public speaker, I promote myself and my agenda around the world regardless of what I'm doing, even if I'm sleeping. What do I mean by this? Well, many of my speeches are recorded and used additional times by the groups sponsoring my events. I speak just once, but the marketing benefit occurs every time someone new listens to the recording online. Once I write an article, thousands of hard copies float in circulation. Most articles are also placed on the Internet, where anyone can read them at any time.

A recurring theme of this book is that you need to establish an area of expertise and craft a message about it that would appeal to your personal target audience. I've developed an expertise in real estate, economic development and career success. Because of that, I now get paid to write and receive honoraria when I speak. You can too.

Anyone can become a writer or a speaker and use these activities for self marketing gain. You need to establish an area of expertise, master the fundamentals of good writing or speaking, and then figure out how to find gigs. Then, just take the initiative and get started.

The balance of this chapter is dedicated to helping you be a success, spreading your message via the word processor and the microphone.

WRITING

The writer Robert Benchley once said, "The freelance writer is a man who is paid per piece, per word or perhaps." In other words, you don't do it for the money, at least not when you are beginning. Instead of thinking of writing as a profit center, think of it as a personal calling card. If you write enough articles, people start to notice you and eventually respect you as an accomplished, well-known expert.

You can become a published writer through a number of venues. Most cities have a host of local publications, some of which are highly specialized. I write a column on economic development for a weekly tabloid newspaper that prints about 15,000 copies a week.

Countless professionals write newspaper or magazine columns based on their expertise. Darren Obrecht, an investment adviser I know quite well, writes columns in magazines and newspapers, giving readers investment information. Earlier in his career, he had his own financial talk show. That's obviously a self marketing benefit for him but also a source of valuable information for the readers.

If you hope to use writing as a form of self marketing, you have a number of options. You could write a column on your area of expertise, or you could work as a general writer, covering a wide variety of topics. Obviously, the advantage of writing a column based on your profession cements your good reputation among potential clients. Writing general articles allows you to expose your name and work to a more diverse population. It also means that you will interview a wide variety of people from varying industries, which could further help you identify professional opportunities.

As a new writer, it will be a challenge getting published that first time, but once you "break the dam," future writing opportunities will flow. I've done enough writing that occasionally I've had to turn down offers for lack of time.

I started writing several years ago, when *Midwest Real Estate News*, a Chicago-based real estate trade magazine, invited me to do an article summarizing real estate development activity in Omaha. A few months later, that same magazine had a temporary staff shortage and was facing a deadline. Because they liked the work I did on the first article, they asked me if I would write a feature on the franchising trend in commercial real estate. I accepted the offer.

To prepare for the article, I interviewed top executives in three international real estate franchising companies. I also interviewed several owners of local real estate companies that had affiliated with national brands. The result was a comprehensive article that garnered quite a bit of positive attention for me.

As I enjoyed the success of that article, it dawned on me that I should be doing this all the time as a way to enhance name recognition and generate clients for my company. I scheduled a lunch meeting with the editor of a local weekly alternative paper. I pitched the possibility of a regular column that covered real estate development in the city. Much to my disappointment, he rejected my offer, claiming I had a conflict of interest. I tried to change his mind but couldn't get anywhere.

Undeterred, I contacted the *Midlands Business Journal* and offered to write general stories. I wrote for this weekly business newspaper for about two years. Eventually, that led to an opportunity to have my own column in *The City Weekly*. In the meantime, I wrote several additional articles for an assortment of newspapers and magazines.

Many self marketers take on a much bigger task than writing articles: They write entire books. From personal experience, I can tell you it's a hell of a lot easier to write a bunch of articles than one book. However, if you have a good idea, a lot of stamina and are disciplined enough to write at least a little bit every day for several months, a book is the granddaddy of all ways to self market.

More and more successful business people are using books as "business cards." A respected professional can write a book and hand it out to prospective clients, hoping to impress them. There's something very respectable about writing a book. Whenever I talk to someone who went to the trouble of doing extensive research, organized it and tediously communicated it in a bound volume, I am instantly impressed. In my mind, I respect that person as an expert, an authority. If you have the will to take on such a major task, a book is the end-all-be-all method of writing your way out of obscurity.

If you want to gain name recognition and build a positive reputation through writing, be prepared for a lot of hard work. Most writing assignments don't pay anything at all. Those that do pay are very insignificant. After factoring all your time, you generally make about minimum wage.

There are several steps to writing. You must think of a topic or be assigned one by an editor. Next, you must identify sources that would be relevant and impressive to the reader. Convincing your sources to do interviews with you can be challenging. Many people are wary of the media. Even as a part-time freelancer, you are "THE MEDIA" in the eyes of an interviewee. It helps to explain to them that you are a business person first and a writer second. I've noticed this puts sources at ease. They like knowing you are "one of them."

You must take copious notes during interviews. If you quote someone, you have an ethical obligation to make sure you write their words verbatim. To make life a little easier, some writers email interview questions to their sources. The source simply types the answers and then emails the response back to the sender. This saves time and increases the likelihood that quotes will be accurate.

As you compose the article, put yourself in your typical reader's shoes. You have to make sure that someone who knows nothing about the subject, who quickly browses the article, can understand the message you're trying to convey.

Whether you write news articles, feature stories or opinion pieces, your articles should follow the same basic rules of journalistic writing we discussed in the previous chapter regarding press releases. Remember the inverted pyramid style. Use lead sentences and write in the active voice as much as possible. Your writing should follow Associated Press (AP) style.

Unless you are writing for a publication you created yourself, you give up some control once you submit the article. An editor will probably review your work and make at least a few minor changes. For the most part, having an editor is a blessing. It reduces the likelihood of embarrassing mistakes.

There has to be "balance" between your editor and you. Don't allow the editor to walk all over you and change too much, but be understanding and remember the editor has a job to do. The relationship between an editor and a writer should be like a good marriage: Both have to give a little.

PUBLIC SPEAKING

Being an effective public speaker is a powerful self marketing tool. As mentioned earlier, I deliver a number of speeches each year. These have allowed me to build name recognition and acquire clients for my real estate business.

Experienced speakers make speech making look almost effortless, but it is hard work. It requires training and commitment. The famous playwright Oscar Wilde said, "Lots of people act well, but few people talk well. This shows that talking is the more difficult of the two."

After delivering hundreds of speeches in my career, it's almost second nature. Sure, it still takes preparation time, and I still have to muster a lot of energy in order to keep the audience engaged, but it is much easier now than when I first started.

A lot of speakers are awkward and uncomfortable when they are just beginners. For many people, their first and only experience with public speaking came during those awkward school speeches they had to give to their fellow students in English class.

I'll never forget one of my first speeches at Valley View Junior High School. Our assignment in English class was to give a five-minute "demonstration" speech. Basically, we were required to show the audience how to do something. After much contemplation, I chose my topic: "How to Sand Wood." I can't remember how or why I came up with such a riveting topic.

To a shy, undersized seventh grader, *speech* is about the scariest word in the dictionary. I fretted for days about getting in front of the whole class. I practiced several times the night before and got my speech up to the required five minutes.

The next day, my heart was pounding and my mouth was dry as I walked to the podium. My hands were shaking so badly I had a hard time holding the damned wood I was supposed to be sanding. As I finished my oration, I breathed a huge sigh of relief, looked at my stopwatch and realized my speech used up a grand total of one minute and 23 seconds.

From humble beginnings, I've come a long way. Public speaking is rather easy now. Occasionally, I'll still get tinges of nervousness especially if it's a new topic, if I'm not feeling well or if the audience is comprised of people I am particularly hoping to impress.

I've evolved to the point where I am actually better at public speaking than interpersonal conversation. Frankly, I find public speaking to be more comfortable than having a one-on-one conversation with someone I don't know very well.

With the right outlook and a great deal of practice, public speaking is an enjoyable experience. It can be very rewarding. The end of a speech is a real buzz. Few things in life are more enjoyable than the high you get when an audience gives you a hearty round of applause following a well-delivered speech.

Good speakers follow "The Three Es Rule": Speakers exist to 1. Educate; 2. Entertain; and 3. Energize an audience. While your true motivation for delivering a speech might be to market yourself or your business, you must come across as if your sole reason is to benefit the audience. Attendees at a speech don't really care about you or your company; they care about themselves, their time, their education and their entertainment.

Unfortunately, only a small percentage of public speakers are truly good. The political leader Adlai E. Stevenson lamented the dearth of public-speaking talent when he said, "I sometimes marvel at the extraordinary docility with which Americans submit to speeches."

While audience members may be docile during a bad speech, chances are they will never attend a second presentation by a poor speaker. To make public speaking a worthwhile self marketing endeavor, you MUST be good.

How do you become good? For one thing, it takes discipline. You have to be committed to growing and developing as a public speaker. That requires you to put time and resources into it.

I have known many professionals who have joined a Toastmasters International club. Toastmasters meet regularly to help each other improve their speaking skills. Each member takes a turn as the speaker while the others serve as audience members. Following the speech, members can give constructive criticism.

Other professionals have enrolled in public speaking classes at local colleges or universities. There are also one-day seminars and sessions during conventions. You can learn in the privacy of your own home or office by purchasing self-instruction DVDs.

If you don't mind spending some money, you can hire a speaking coach. This is essentially like taking private lessons. Speaking coaches will likely put you through a number of drills to help you improve. They may also have you speak into a camera and then play back your performance, so you can critique yourself.

Whatever method you use to improve your speaking, ultimately nothing teaches you more than "on-the-job training." After you have studied *how* to be a good speaker, get out and *do* it. To improve, have someone videotape your presentation. Also ask a trusted friend or colleague to take notes for you. Anytime you do something good or bad, your friend should write it down and share it with you during a post-speech critique. There is no better way to learn than critiquing a real performance.

DEALING WITH STAGE FRIGHT

Stage fright is a very natural part of public speaking, but you need to know how to handle it. Some nervousness is a good thing, because it pushes us to prepare, concentrate and do a good job. When you run the risk of embarrassing yourself in front of a large group of people, you are likely to focus on the task and do your best.

Unchecked stage fright, however, can be paralyzing. I have used a number of techniques over the years to help me deal with it.

First of all, accept stage fright as a fact of life. The first few times you speak, you will be nervous. As you become more experienced, most nervousness will subside. For your first speech, just stand up and force yourself to do it. Once you start speaking and get a few sentences out, the nervousness usually fades away.

If your heart is pounding and your lungs are breathing rapidly as you approach the podium, take a few moments before you jump into your script. Straighten your papers, adjust the microphone, thank the person who introduced you and say something nice about him or her. Look out at the audience and smile before you begin talking. This small sequence of events can help you catch your breath and settle into speaking mode.

If you are inexperienced as a speaker, be careful about jokes. A lot of people will advise you, "Tell a joke at the beginning; it loosens up the crowd and calms the speaker's nerves." That's true as long as the joke is actually funny. A bad joke during a speech is received about as well as a fart in church. If you are not positive your joke is funny, and that you are capable of delivering it properly, don't do it. Nothing flusters an inexperienced speaker more than a joke that bombs.

There's also the age-old advice: "Pretend the audience members are all wearing underwear." I can't say that I've ever done this, but I like the spirit and intent of this advice. In other words, audience members are only human. They have as many or more problems and inadequacies as you do. Don't build them into some monolithic gathering of super beings. Most of them would be nervous too if they were in your shoes.

I received some good advice when I first started as a radio personality. It applies to public speaking as well. Pretend you are talking to one person you know very well. It could be a spouse, your parent, your boyfriend, whoever. This personalizes the audience. For most people, it's much easier to talk to a trusted friend instead of a room full of strangers.

It helps to get a little cocky. Remind yourself that the audience is there to see and hear YOU. That means you are doing them a favor. You are providing them with education, entertainment and energy they do not currently have. They are lucky you are willing to take your valuable time to give it to them.

It helps to use confident body language regardless of how nervous you may be. When I am introduced as a speaker, I stand up and walk confidently toward the podium. I look the introducer in the eye and give him or her a firm handshake. It's hard to explain why, but an outward show of confidence helps me feel more confident on the inside too.

Don't panic if you lose your place or if you become short of breath during the speech. Simply pause until you find your place. To the speaker, pauses seem 10 times longer than they really are. Actually, pauses are important speaking tools. They break up the monotony and can wake up a drifting audience member.

I find it helpful to think about the end when I am uncomfortable giving a speech. With each sentence you utter, you move closer to the end reward – the applause. Remind yourself that your hard work, concentration and endurance of stage fright all pay off when the speech is done.

Much of your potential stage fright can be prevented before you even arrive at the speaking venue. First, prepare well. The more you prepare, the more confident you are about your material. Second, as the old saying goes, practice makes perfect. Practice not only makes your speech better, it makes you more comfortable. The day before a speech, drive to the venue. Simply seeing the place and knowing the route to get there can put your mind at ease.

Make sure you arrive at the venue early. If you are weaving in and out of traffic desperately trying to beat the clock, you will be flustered before you even get there. Arriving early allows you to chit-chat with audience members ahead of time. This helps you to bond with audience members and serves to "warm you up" before going on stage.

Finally, take some time the day before or the morning of the speech to "visualize" success. It is common for football coaches to have their athletes imagine themselves making great plays. I believe in the power of positive visualization and use it frequently. When I am driving to any important event in which I have to perform or accomplish something, I imagine myself being confident, knowledgeable and successful. Try it sometime. It really works.

THE BASICS OF PUBLIC SPEAKING

There are entire college courses offered on public speaking, but you can learn enough to be effective by remembering the basic rules. Keep these basics in mind as you write your script or outline and as you deliver your remarks.

First, be interesting. Nobody wants to listen to a boring speech. Second, be relevant. Nobody wants to listen to a pointless speech. It's a good idea to come up with something different or a new angle the audience has never heard. Spend time during script writing to come up with something that will engage the audience. Otherwise they'll leave the event resenting you for wasting their time.

Stand up straight and be confident when you are in front of a room. You don't have to stand at attention like the guys who guard Queen Elizabeth's palace, but you should look strong, confident and alert. Don't slouch.

I'm not recommending you act like a high school cheerleader, but it is important to be energetic, positive and optimistic. Audience members want to be motivated and empowered by speakers. They want to feel good about something following the presentation. Even if you are presenting ominous information and warning the audience about something, you should always end on a positive, optimistic note.

Not only was Abraham Lincoln a great leader, he was a master orator. Despite a shrill voice, Lincoln was captivating when speaking from the stump. His speeches engaged audiences so well in part because Lincoln was a master storyteller. He wove stories and analogies into his speeches. He used stories to bring his speeches to life. Storytelling made it easier for everyday citizens to understand what would otherwise be dry policy lectures or political speeches.

I try to emulate Lincoln and history's other great orators in my speaking. I have found storytelling to be a highly effective tool. I try to weave in a handful of vignettes into each presentation. Not only do the stories help me get my point across, they keep the audience entertained. That's especially important when you are giving an afternoon speech immediately following lunch. Stories will keep people from literally falling asleep during your presentation.

Another way to wake up the sleepy heads in your audience is to subtly change your voice volume and make different voice inflections throughout the presentation. I also recommend a strategic pause. I like to pause right before a punch line or as I lead up to a particularly important point.

Speakers have to work hard to get a good laugh. When you get one, take a moment to bask in the glory.

If the audience laughs at your joke, pause before you resume your speech. If you talk over the laugh, you risk two things: Part of what you say won't be heard, and you could cut off their laughing prematurely. Believe me, the more the audience laughs, the better your speech will be perceived. Speakers have to work hard to get a good laugh. When you get one, take a moment to bask in the glory.

The use of humor helps as long as it's truly funny. If you are one of those speakers who always messes up the delivery of a punch line, you're better off not trying. Also, situational humor, related to your topic, is generally better received than a canned joke someone told you on the bus.

A self-deprecating joke is one of the best uses of humor in a speech. When you poke fun at yourself, it tells the audience that you're a down-to-earth person who is pleasant to hang out with. It shows some humility. Be careful, however, because there is an art to self-deprecating humor. You don't want to do it too much, or it appears that you are actually begging for a compliment. I know of a U.S. Senator who always includes several self-deprecating comments in his speeches. It's painful to listen to because everyone knows he has a massive ego. It's just too much. His repeated self-deprecating humor gets old and doesn't seem genuine.

You should always maintain some decorum of formality in your presentations. If you get too laid back and casual, it doesn't seem like a speech. The audience may feel as if you are not respecting them if you get too informal.

It's important to avoid blatantly offensive comments. In this day of runaway political correctness, it's impossible not to offend anyone, but you should avoid saying anything racist, sexist, ageist or obscene. Don't bash on a religion. For many people, their religion has deep personal meaning to them. Avoid four-letter words, especially the "big" ones like the F-word. While most adults can handle hearing these words, using them is simply not professional.

When presenting, you may be tempted to speak in innuendos and tell inside jokes. Although some audience members might find that quite funny, a lot of them won't get it. That makes them feel left out, thus damaging the tie you are trying to create between them and you.

You should use good grammar. As a speaker, you are being quietly judged by everyone in the audience. Audience members can be cruel and harsh critics. One of the fastest ways to lose their respect is to use poor grammar in your presentation. If you're using public speaking as a self marketing tool, don't ruin its effectiveness by sounding uneducated and unsophisticated.

When you stand in front of an audience, speak confidently and project your voice. If you ever took singing lessons or participated in a choir, you probably remember being taught to "sing from your diaphragm." Such advice likewise applies to public speaking. Take full breaths so that your voice is backed by a lot of air. Breathe by expanding your abdomen, not your chest. Full breathing carries your voice to each audience member's ears. If you truly use your diaphragm (the large muscle in the abdomen, which makes breathing possible), you should be able speak effectively without a microphone.

If you do use a microphone, make sure your microphone mechanics are sound. Just because you have a microphone doesn't mean you can whisper. Good microphone technique still requires you to use your diaphragm and project your voice into the sound system. Usually, you want your mouth to be about five or six inches from the mike. Avoid over pronouncing "s" sounds when using a mike, and make sure you don't cough or clear your throat into the microphone. That's a very annoying audio experience for your audience.

If the microphone is hooked up to a podium, do not leave the podium. Some speakers will periodically stray from the podium. As soon as they do, their voices are lost. If the venue makes a wireless microphone available to you, feel free to move about. Movement helps keep the audience alert. Just be careful not to move too erratically or nervously. That's a distraction. Before and after your speech, make sure your wireless microphone is off. You don't want to leave it on accidentally and have the entire hall hear your private comments.

As your teacher likely emphasized during high school English class speeches, you need to make eye contact with the audience. This personally connects the audience to you and keeps them interested. It also makes audience members feel important enough that the speaker looks them squarely in the eye. It's okay to look at your notes; just be sure to look up regularly and make contact with your listeners.

Like eye contact, the use of hand gestures also keeps the audience alert. Hand gestures are particularly effective when you want to emphasize a key point. Just be careful that you don't wave your hands around without purpose. Using too many meaningless gestures is hard on the audience members' eyes.

My advice on using facial expressions is similar to what I said about hand gestures. It is important but can be overdone. Practice facial expressions in the mirror at home, so you know exactly how each facial expression looks before you use it. Facial expressions can be particularly useful auxiliaries to humor.

Speak clearly throughout your presentation. If you are a "mumbler," you need to get over it. Enunciate each word clearly. Notice how broadcasters on television and radio speak. Think about the way they carefully pronounce each syllable. Generally, that's the way you should speak during a speech.

Avoid using meaningless filler words such as *uhm*, *like* and *you know*. There is like nothing, like more annoying than like a speaker, who, like, keeps saying the same word, like over and over again, you know?

Some speakers have a tendency to over rely on one word. For most speakers, this is a habit they probably do not realize they have. I know a football coach who uses the word *tremendous* multiple times whenever he gives a speech or does interviews with the media. I remember one speaker who used the word *beautiful* in darned near every sentence of her speech. Instead of learning from her, audience members were counting how many times she used *beautiful*. She continued to use it during the question-and-answer session following the speech.

When crafting your script, think about the "Rule of 3s." Three is a magic number in the public speaking world. For some reason, audiences respond better when speeches are broken into three parts or you have three arguments for each point. This is why you often hear speakers say things such as: "I will prove this by illustrating three main points," or "We are seeing three primary trends in the industry today."

Great speakers tend to emphasize the most critical messages three times. As the great orator and statesman Winston Churchill said, "If you have an important point to make, don't try to be subtle or clever. Use the pile driver. Hit the point once. Then come back and hit it again. Then hit it a third time; a tremendous whack."

All speakers must face the visual-aid dilemma: Do you use them or not? There are pros and cons to using visual aids. These can be props, large physical items you show the audience to prove a point, a video, audio recording or PowerPoint slide show. Be careful that you do not overdo it. If the visual aid does not directly enhance the speech, it is probably just a distraction.

PowerPoint is a wonderful tool if you employ it properly. Unfortunately, it may be the single most destructive force in public speaking today. PowerPoint can ruin a good speech, making it boring and tedious. This may come as a surprise to you, but just because technology is available doesn't mean you have to use it.

Too many times speakers with a PowerPoint presentation do nothing but read what the slides say. How torturously boring for the audience! If you're going to read the slides, just give everyone a printout of the PowerPoint slides and let everyone go home early. If you're going to use this technology, find some way to integrate it seamlessly into the presentation. Don't stand with your back to the audience, holding up your remote control while monotonously reading what's on your slides. A seasoned, enlightening and entertaining speaker does not need any visual aids whatsoever.

When writing your speech, you need to strike a balance. On one hand, you must be descriptive to adequately explain your point. On the other hand, it is easy to slip into the dark side and become too verbose. Try to convey a great deal of meaning in few words.

Carefully plan the structure of your speech. Like a good novel, a speech should have a climax located somewhere near the end but not quite at the end. Outstanding script writers will build the text, bringing up the audience's level of interest until the climax, where the most exciting part of the message is delivered.

Your ending should be uplifting, emphatic, motivational, and should call the audience to action. The end is very important. Most people have relatively short attention spans. That means they are likely to drift off every now and then during the meat of your speech. Audience members, however, can sense when the speech is drawing to a close. Their minds are in a much greater state of arousal near the end. Use that to your advantage by placing some important stuff at or just after the climax.

SELF MARKETING

A speaker can maximize a speech's self marketing benefit in many ways. As a speaker, one of your most important missions is to build rapport between the audience and you. The more they like you, the greater your self marketing benefit will be.

One way to do this is to arrive early to greet and shake hands with your audience members. This personalizes and humanizes you. They are more likely to follow your speech closely if they have a connection to you. Likewise, stay after the speech to meet, greet and answer one-on-one questions. This is the most valuable part of the entire speaking performance from a self-marketing perspective. This is the time when audience members come up to ask questions, exchange business cards and talk about ideas and opportunities. Don't miss out on this important time by skipping out as soon as you say "thank you."

Long before the speech, write your own introduction and give it to the person who booked you. Make sure he or she knows that the introduction should be read verbatim.

I have noticed that without a written introduction, almost every introducer messes up something about my background. They'll mispronounce the name of my company. They may leave out a key part of my background that justifies why I'm speaking on the topic. I've had people say my last name was "Beal" or "Fields" instead of "Beals." I've been introduced as "Chuck" or "Jack" instead of "Jeff." The name of my company, Coldwell Banker Commercial World Group, is rather cumbersome. I can't count the ways introducers have butchered that. My all-time favorite is "Coldwell's World Bank."

Being introduced improperly is obviously counterproductive to your self marketing goals.

During your speech, tactfully work in some information about you, your company or your cause, whatever is applicable. In other words, you are trying to give valuable information and enjoyable entertainment to the audience, but you don't want to miss out on a self marketing opportunity. Just make sure your self-promoting statements are dispersed and not the primary focus of the speech. Otherwise, it comes across as an infomercial.

Most speakers leave time at the end of the presentation for a question-and-answer period. This is a good idea, because it allows direct interaction between presenter and listener. It also guarantees that unanswered questions see the light of day. Don't ask for questions too soon. Give the people a speech first; then solicit questions. I've attended presentations where the speaker will say just a couple things and then open it for questions. This approach makes you look unprepared, tired and disinterested. Remember, people want to be entertained by a speaker.

Don't allow audience members to interrupt you during your speech with questions. It's incredibly rude, but some people have no problem doing it. If someone raises a hand or cuts you off during your speech, simply say. "I appreciate the question. I'd like to get through my presentation first, and then I'll open it up to everyone's questions." The speaker is the leader and must maintain control. If you allow the audience to set the agenda, you tarnish your image.

If you do a good job, you will undoubtedly receive praise following the speech. Accept it gracefully with sincere gratitude. Anytime someone compliments my speech or my speaking abilities, I simply say, "Thank you. I appreciate that very much." Some people have a tendency to brush it off or downplay the praise. Frankly, that's insulting to the person who gave you the compliment. Don't make audience members feel stupid by minimizing the praise they went out of their way to give you.

GETTING GIGS

Once you have established your area of expertise, developed a script and figured out how to present it properly, the next step is to book your first speech.

The bad news is that it's not always easy to get your first couple of speaking gigs. The good news is that it's very easy to book more gigs after you've successfully done a few speeches.

I have delivered hundreds of speeches over the past few years, and a significant percentage of them have come with honoraria. To get started, you have to find just a couple groups willing to hear you. After that, assuming you do a good job, word of mouth gets you more gigs. I hardly ever advertise my speaking anymore unless I have a new presentation. I have more than enough speaking opportunities to keep me busy simply from referrals. At some points in the year, I have to turn down speaking offers because I'm double-booked.

So how do you get that first speech? For one thing, you can volunteer to give a workshop at a convention or professional association meeting. If you are committed to marketing yourself, you are probably involved in a couple of organizations. See if these organizations would allow you to speak.

When I first developed my speech on Omaha's economic growth and development, I targeted all the service clubs, community groups and professional associations in the city. I prepared an attractive marketing flyer and mailed it to these groups with a cover letter. I found the group names and contact information on the Internet and through my local chamber of commerce. That strategy has led to hundreds of speeches.

Once you book your first speech, bring copies of your marketing flyer and business card to hand out to all the attendees. That will ensure that people have your contact info if they want to book you for a different event. It also makes it easy for audience members to reach you with a business opportunity.

Any self marketer can benefit from public speaking by taking the right steps. At first it seems kind of daunting, because there are so many rules of public speaking that you must remember. Map out a plan that will develop you into a good public speaker and then follow it one step at a time. Before you know it, the view from behind the podium will become quite comfortable for you.

CHAPTER ELEVEN

Anytime, Anywhere: Unleash the Power of the Internet

H ERE'S THE BIGGEST UNDERSTATEMENT OF THE BOOK: THE INTERNET HAS
changed business as we know it. Companies as well as individuals can market themselves efficiently 24 hours a day anywhere in
the world, to an audience of billions. It is still a relatively new communications medium, and although it is already huge, the Internet has the
potential to grow much bigger. Internet marketing is relatively cheap,
and it's the best way to reach the younger members of your personal
target audience.

It's hard to imagine a legitimate company that wouldn't have a website. More and more, the Internet is becoming the primary form of
mass communication for American companies. A significant number of
businesses derive a majority of their sales from their websites.

Because companies find so much benefit from Internet marketing,
does it not make sense that individuals should too? Serious self marketers need to have an Internet presence. Whether it's your own website,

an electronic newsletter, a blog or information about you on someone else's website, you need to have a presence on the World Wide Web.

DISPERSING YOUR NAME

Establishing name recognition is one of the tenets of self marketing. The Internet is a natural way to accomplish that. The Internet allows you to market yourself perpetually when you are at work, at play or even when you're asleep. It is the ultimate multi-tasking tool. Once you establish a presence on a site, you can move on with the rest of your life. The site stays available for viewing by anyone, anytime, anywhere.

When you are just getting started on your Internet name-building effort, it's much easier and cheaper to establish a presence on existing websites than it is to create websites of your own.

Savvy self marketers make sure their names pop up in multiple places when someone searches for them online. If a client Googles your name, you want it to show up on a variety of sites. This gives you legitimacy and tells people that you are a busy, important professional.

If you are a member of a club or organization, encourage the leaders to list member names on the official website. Officers should have bios and pictures on the organization's site. Encourage your employer to do the same. My company includes bios, pictures and contact information on its website for each professional-level employee.

A self marketer needs to establish an expertise in something and then use that as his or her unique promotional hook. Members of your personal target audience love to hear from you if they perceive you as an expert, so doing this carries a great deal of power.

In the previous chapter, we talked about how your expertise can land you speaking and writing gigs. Well, it can also get your name on a variety of websites. Contact websites that pertain to your area of expertise and offer yourself as a source, writer, contributor, professional reference or whatever other excuse you can think of – anything that will get your name on the website. If you work at this hard enough, you will soon have your name littered all over the Internet. You'll know you've been successful when someone you know comes up to you and says, "I Googled your name today, and you showed up everywhere!"

PERSONAL WEBSITE

Once you have established a significant presence on company and organizational websites, it may be time to take your Internet-based self marketing to a higher level: your own website.

Although there is some expense and start-up work involved, you can establish your own site relatively easily. Many companies help individuals or small businesses set up simple websites at a minimal cost.

First, you want to pick your domain name – that's your Internet address. A logical choice would be your own name. Even if you are not ready to launch a site anytime soon, you should buy your own name and any other domain names that relate to you, your business or your personal target audience. For instance, I bought jeffbeals.com years ago, even though I didn't really need it at the time. I simply wanted to reserve it in case I needed it.

To give you an idea of how important Internet domain names are, I actually changed the name of this book just to get a domain name that was available. I originally intended to call it "Self Marketing *Secrets*," but selfmarketingsecrets.com was already taken. I tried to contact the owner of selfmarketingsecrets.com to buy it, but I couldn't reach him. I looked up *www.selfmarketingpower.com*, which I ended up liking better, and found it was available. Voila! The book had a new name.

You can purchase/reserve Internet domain names by going to a registration service such as GoDaddy.com. For a rather small fee, you can protect your future interest in the site names of your choice. In addition to .com, there are additional Internet suffixes you may want to reserve such as .net, .org and .info. There are others as well. If you are serious, buy all the suffixes that go with your name.

If someone already owns your desired name, you might be able to strike a deal to buy it from them. Some people like to "squat" on domain names, hoping to make a profit, so it might cost you. The best idea is to reserve your perfect domain name early before someone else snatches it from you.

Once you have a name and an Internet hosting company, you can create your site. If your goal is self marketing, and your name is your site address, you will probably have a picture, a professional bio and other information about yourself. If you have published articles, put them on there. In fact, a lot of people who have had difficulty convincing established periodicals to publish their writing will use their own Internet sites to publish their work.

MORE INTERNET COMMUNICATION

Establishing a personal site is a vital step, but it's only the first basic step. Websites by themselves are rather passive. A visitor comes to the site, reads your stuff and then leaves – maybe never comes back. If, however, you have interactive features or regularly changing material, you can get visitors to keep coming back to your site.

Some people create discussion boards related to their area of personal expertise. For instance, we have a discussion board on our *Grow Omaha* radio program website. Anyone who is interested in our show format can register on our discussion board and communicate online with people who share the same interest.

Many self marketers are turning to weblogs to get their messages out on their own sites. Also known as "blogs," these are online diaries that you can make public or available to a select audience. To be successful, blogs need to be regularly updated so that readers have a reason to keep returning, thus keeping your name and ideas at the front of their minds. Some self marketers create blogs as part of a personal website. Others go through a blog design and hosting service.

Although blogs tend to be rather informal, you may want to have a more professional, formal communication tool. That's where electronic newsletters come in. E-newsletters are more journalistic than blogs because they report facts and present well-written commentary based on your expertise. If you write and design these newsletters effectively, and then aggressively market them, they can become surprisingly popular.

It is not hard to create a sign-in feature on your website where visitors can voluntarily place their email addresses on your e-newsletter blast list. If you don't do a full-blown newsletter, perhaps you will promote yourself and communicate your expertise through daily, weekly or monthly updates.

For listeners of my radio show, I email a quarterly newsletter and weekly updates. After three years, I have built my distribution list up to almost 5,000 subscribers. That means once a week, thousands of people get an email with my name, the name of my show and my carefully crafted message. It's a powerful marketing tool for the show.

A number of companies offer Internet-based software programs to help you create and manage your blast emails. I use Constant Contact, Inc., for mine. Based in Massachusetts, Constant Contact allows you to create a distribution list comprised of your target audience and then gives you several templates from which you can craft nice-looking blast emails. About 100,000 small businesses and organizations use this service, and the prices are quite reasonable. You can reach the company at constantcontact.com.

If you do blast emails of newsletters, weekly updates, or advertisements for your products and services, send them on a Tuesday, Wednesday or Thursday. The weekends are bad, because too many people are away from the office. Mondays and Fridays are bad, because your readers are either shaking off the old weekend or mentally preparing for the next. The best time of day for sending blast emails is mid-morning or early afternoon. Avoid the lunch hour as well as the very beginning or end of the day.

PODCASTS

If you have ever wanted to broadcast your voice to listeners around the world but you don't own your own network of radio stations, there is an option for you: podcasting. According to Tee Morris, one of the gurus of this relatively new phenomenon, podcasting is actually a spin-off of blogging.

Podcasting combines blogging with audio files that can be played on your desktop or downloaded onto your MP3 player and taken with you. Unlike scheduled broadcasts on the radio, you can listen to podcasts at any time anywhere in the world.

Podcasting is a relatively inexpensive way for you to get your audio material in front of a worldwide audience. There are a couple challenges however. First, your material needs to be good. No one is going to listen to garbage just because it's easy to download. Second, you have to market it in order to get an audience. The Internet is huge and incredibly fragmented. It's very easy for your podcast to get lost in the clutter.

In order to be relevant, you'll have to market the heck out of your podcast. In that spirit, however, several podcasts have turned into big-time successes. Something about them has made them catch on like wildfire and capture huge audiences. Imagine what a powerful podcast could do for your career.

INTERNET NETWORKING

Networking is the grassroots of self marketing. It is one of the easiest and most effective forms of building name recognition and building a list of influential contacts. Although you never want to abandon face-to-face networking, the Internet provides a number of virtual networking opportunities that can supplement your flesh-pressing efforts.

LinkedIn is one example. This California-based dot.com has millions of subscribers in virtually every country in the world and is adding 130,000 new people each week. LinkedIn allows you to take your professional networking online, giving you access to people, jobs and information. It capitalizes on the interconnectivity of the Internet to hook you up with past colleagues with whom you may have lost contact and new ones who share your interests. A free service, it is the world's largest professional network. Not only is it useful for business, it's also a lot of fun reading profiles of people you once knew or would like to meet.

Whatever tool or website you use, the important message is to take your networking efforts online. Self marketing should be a multi-media campaign. You need to use every tool available. Internet-based networking just happens to be one of the most efficient tools.

RESEARCH TOOL

While you should use the Internet to promote yourself and build name recognition, let us not forget what a powerful research tool the Internet is. Let us also remember that in the information age, we are expected to be up-to-date at all times. With so much information at our fingertips, there is no excuse not to be fully informed.

In addition to keeping up with current affairs and the news inside your industry, the Internet allows you to research individual people – the people who are part of your personal target audience. If you are meeting with an important client, you should research the client online. You will be much more likely to impress this potential business client if you already know the person's background and interests. This knowledge will better allow you to steer the conversation toward the client's passions. That's a great way to build rapport and get the client to like you.

You may also uncover enough information online to know what to avoid when meeting with someone. Assume your competitors are fully exploiting the power of the Internet and make sure you do the same. You don't want to give up any advantages to a competitor just because you failed to read critical information that is available at the click of a mouse.

It's interesting how the readily available information on the Internet has made research so easy. I teach a college course in which the students are required to write a term paper. When I was in college, term papers required me to spend hours combing stacks of academic books housed in a massive university library with more than 2 million volumes. Today, my students can find scholarly journal articles online. It's changed so much that my students don't even go to the library unless it is to visit the trendy little coffee shop there.

CHAPTER TWELVE

Think Like
a Marketer

ECAUSE YOU ARE A BUSINESS UNTO YOURSELF WITH YOUR OWN BRAND TO promote, it is only logical that you should think like a marketer. Personal brands are symbolic embodiments of a self marketer that publicly distinguish that person from all other competitors. A brand is a trademark, a distinctive name, and a combination of images that creates associations and expectations in the minds of audience members.

Marketers of products and services are obsessed with branding. Companies hire talented marketers to craft strategic plans for each of their brands and then carry out the communications tactics that are part of the plans.

Likewise, you need a strategic plan and a tactical communications system for your personal brand. Fortunately, your strategic self marketing plan can be much simpler and require far less quantitative research than a typical corporate marketing plan. As a self marketer, you should be obsessed with your personal brand.

The purpose of a strategic self marketing plan is to build name recognition and positive opinions about your personal brand so that members of your personal target audience think of you when they have some personal or business opportunity that you would like.

If you have never developed a personal strategic plan before, you are in for a healthy mental exercise. By creating a plan, looking back at it regularly and tweaking it each year, you will likely accelerate your success substantially. Strategic planning never ends. It is a process that is often changed and renewed as your career progresses.

You will need to take several steps in order to establish your strategic self marketing plan.

VISION STATEMENT

One of the first steps in your plan is to craft a vision statement. This is a snapshot of where you hope to be at some point in the future. In self marketing, the vision statement is what you will be like professionally and how your life will be better after succeeding in your self marketing efforts. As far as the actual writing is concerned, your vision statement should be clear, concise and not very long. You want to keep it short and easy to read so that you can effortlessly keep going back to it for reminder and motivation purposes.

A self marketing vision statement could read something like this: "To become the most recognized financial planning expert in my community" or "To increase my name recognition every year as I become the top real estate agent in the city."

TARGET AUDIENCE

Six-and-a-half billion is an overwhelming number. That's how many people live on this planet. If you had to market to all of them, you would have an impossible task. The good news is that you don't have to worry about everyone. You only need to impress a very specific and narrow slice of the population

One of the most important steps of strategic self marketing planning is to determine your personal target audience. This is the group of people to whom your self marketing message is directed. You identify those whom you most need to impress and focus your attention on them. Determination of your personal target audience is influenced by what your purpose and vision are for self marketing. If you are running for an elected office, your personal target audience would consist of voters in your precinct and those who influence voters. If you are trying to land a better job, your target audience would be potential employers, reference givers and people who could help you network with the right decision makers.

In general, life-long self marketing, your personal target audience is going to be much broader than these examples. These would be anyone who could conceivably be a client, a referral, a boss or a friend.

ASSESSMENT

After you have determined your vision statement, you need to assess the current situation. This involves looking at the people with whom you are competing as well as looking inward at yourself.

Let's address the other people first. Serious self marketers take time in developing their plan to do a competitive analysis. In this exercise, look at other self marketers who have the same target audience you have, are in a similar profession or have similar socio-political goals. Think about all they do well and all they do poorly. How do you stack up against them in each category you study? Be honest and write down true answers. Don't be too hard on yourself, but don't turn a blind eye to any competitive reality you really need to address.

The SWOT analysis is a key part of the assessment process. "SWOT" is an acronym for "Strengths, Weaknesses, Opportunities, Threats." SWOT analyses are easy and actually fun to do. Take four pieces of paper (or do it on a spreadsheet program). At the top of each sheet, write one of the four words that comprise the acronym "SWOT."

Under Strengths, list every single thing you can think of about yourself that is a strength vis-à-vis other self marketers. Go through the same exercise with Weaknesses, Opportunities and Threats. What external opportunities could propel your self marketing effectiveness? What are the external threats that could be detrimental? When going through this exercise, it is critical that you be completely honest. Don't build yourself up higher than you are, but don't discount yourself unnecessarily when doing your SWOT.

Your personal SWOT analysis is a revealing exercise. You can use it as a starting point for determining goals and other aspects of your plan. Everything you do from here on should capitalize on your strengths and opportunities while minimizing your weaknesses and threats.

GOALS AND OBJECTIVES

As you set goals and objectives for your career and life in general, make sure some of them focus on self marketing efforts. Goals and objectives should spring from your strategic marketing plan's purpose and vision.

Goals and objectives should be in writing and as quantitative and specific as possible. The better your goals, the more effective your self marketing will be. We will explore goal setting much more deeply in chapter 15.

In the goals and objectives section of your plan, you might list how you will build name recognition and develop a positive reputation.

OPERATIONS STRATEGY

You are now ready to operationalize your personal marketing strategic plan. We do this by incorporating a number of marketing tactics such as publicity, advertising and networking.

Publicity is unpaid media communication, often called "earned" media. We discussed how to get publicity in chapters 9 and 10.

Advertising is paid media communication. Most self marketers don't do a lot of advertising because it's expensive and has too much of a shotgun approach. In other words, when you buy an advertisement in the mass media, you are paying for and communicating to a large, broad, diverse audience, when you really want a narrower audience. Nevertheless, some self marketers have occasionally found themselves in situations when advertising made sense for them.

As discussed in chapter 8, networking is the grassroots of self marketing. Although networking comes across as a casual, relaxed activity, it needs to be planned in order to be most effective. In your strategic self marketing plan, think of specific ways in which your networking can be effective. Identify the types of events at which you will network, who you will try to meet and how you will go about doing it.

Regardless of the communication tactics you employ to carry out your plan, remember to be honest. Companies deservedly feel the heat when they engage in deceptive advertising. Likewise, you should never be deceptive in your personal promotion activities. The short-term gain you get from it will be outweighed by the long-term harm you will be doing.

While deceptive self marketing is bad, it is generally okay to use a little bit of puffery and some euphemisms in your communications. Puffery is a slight exaggeration of fact done in such a way that nobody considers it lying. For example, you might call yourself, "the friendliest insurance agent in the state." No matter how nice you are, that's probably not true. Anyone who thinks about it can figure out that it's just puffery. Calling yourself a "guru" could be an acceptable euphemism assuming you are an expert in your field.

BASIC MARKETING PRINCIPLES

Some laws in marketing are worth considering. Among these are the laws of frequency, repetition and prioritization.

Frequency and repetition matter a great deal. In order for the typical person to remember your name, he or she needs to hear it over and over again. What's more, exposure to your name and reputation needs to occur consistently on a perpetual basis.

As consumers of information, we need to hear the same thing many times and in many instances in order for it to become fully rooted in our brains. That's why you hear company names repeated so many times in commercials and why the same commercials are played over and over. It's why successful companies continue to advertise even after they've been around for years and have established large customer bases.

Spend more resources on the ones who can help you most.

Self marketers must never let down. They have to keep showing up at public events and scheduling meetings with people. They need to keep getting publicity and engaging in high-profile activities. If you fall out of the self marketing spotlight for just a short time, your star fades rapidly.

Prioritization means that you spend the majority of your self marketing time focusing on that part of your personal target audience that has the highest likelihood of benefiting you. Now, it's wise to market yourself to everyone, keeping in mind that opportunity sometimes comes from the least likely sources, but you should spend more resources on the ones who can help you most. Furthermore, you spend more time on those people who are the closest to giving you an opportunity than you would to someone you just met.

Like all forms of marketing, self marketing is a numbers game. You might have to send out 50 resumés just to land one job. You might have to make 100 phone calls to land one client. You may have to network with 100 people before you are offered a major-league opportunity.

THE FUNNEL

To illustrate how marketing is a numbers game that requires prioritization skills, let's take a moment to think about the classic marketing funnel.

Picture a big funnel like something you would use to pour oil into an automobile engine. Instead of serving as a conduit for liquid, however, the marketing funnel is a conduit for turning prospects into clients.

At the top of any marketing funnel would be all prospects in the world. As you go down the funnel, the opening narrows, meaning there is less space for prospects. Each step in the marketing process requires you to go farther down into the funnel. Since there is less space at each step in the funnel, there are fewer prospects. At the very bottom of the funnel, only a few prospects actually drip out. Those that do represent the ones that become actual customers.

I'll further explain the marketing funnel and how it pertains to self marketing by describing a job-search funnel and a client-acquisition funnel.

In the job-search funnel, you have all possible employers at the top. A little ways down, you have the employers you actually meet. Next are those employers who actually receive your resumé. Those with whom you interview are farther down the funnel. At the very bottom of the funnel would be the employer who offered you a job.

In the client-acquisition funnel, you have all prospective clients at the broad top of the funnel. Other steps moving down from the top toward the narrower part would include those who hear about you through personal or mass media communication; those you meet through networking; those who hear your formal presentation; those who visit your office for a follow-up meeting; and those you engage in hard-core negotiations. Finally, the clients who actually sign up represent the drops falling out of the funnel's narrow base.

The funnel is important because it reinforces a couple very important things to remember. Number one, you will be dealing with prospects at all points in your funnel at any given time. That said, you should devote more time per prospect to those who are farther down.

Second, when you meet a new prospect, a "top-of-the-funnel person," don't worry about turning him or her into a closed deal right away. Your goal with any given person in your funnel should be to advance him or her to the next step. Don't worry about the end; focus on getting the person one step closer to the end.

Third, you must constantly focus on "filling the hopper." While you have to spend more time per person on prospects near the funnel's bottom, you can't forget the top. For instance, salespeople sometimes get so focused on closing big deals that weeks or months will go by when they do no basic prospecting. Therefore, when the deals either close or die off, there is no one left in the upper, broader part of the funnel. The salesperson has failed to fill the hopper while working on the big deals. The same applies to self marketing.

THINK LIKE A REAL ESTATE AGENT

There is a real estate sales concept known as "farming" in which real estate agents choose a geographic area to place particular emphasis. It typically is one neighborhood or subdivision consisting of a few hundred houses.

There's nothing to stop such a real estate agent from doing deals in a variety of neighborhoods throughout the city, but she places particular prospecting focus on the one neighborhood. She memorizes all the houses in that subdivision and tries to get to know all the current owners. She becomes the specialist or expert in that neighborhood. The hope is that anyone thinking of selling a house in the neighborhood would think of the agent and list the house with that expert agent.

Self marketers can learn a lot from real estate "farming." While self marketers probably won't focus on a residential subdivision, there is a lot to be gained by farming your industry or your community.

Real estate agents, as well as salespeople in a variety of other fields, should develop spheres of interest. These would be groups of people they work with, socialize with or share some other common interest. Having a sphere of interest is particularly important for a self marketer.

COMMON SENSE

Ultimately, you need to use common sense in self marketing. If something doesn't feel right, you should ask yourself if it's the right thing to do. While self marketing can be a lot of fun, it takes hard work. After going to the trouble of creating a strategic self marketing plan, don't put it on the shelf to collect dust. Go out into the world and make it become reality.

Self marketing must be a perpetual activity, and you can never let down your intensity. Even when everything in your career and personal life is going great, you need to market yourself in order to be in position for future opportunities.

Responsible people save money to prepare for an unforeseen financial crisis or to be able to invest in a business opportunity that may come their way. Similarly, savvy professionals market themselves to prepare for a rainy day or to take full advantage of a perfect day.

CHAPTER THIRTEEN

Bend All the Rules: Creativity Is Key

THE UNITED STATES SPENT HUNDREDS OF BILLIONS OF DOLLARS ON research and development in 2006, outpacing the European Union and Japan combined.

Despite the massive number of manufacturing jobs lost to China and other developing nations over the past few years, the U.S. economy remains the world's largest by a margin of several trillion dollars.

Despite rapidly increasing competition in the high-tech fields from nations like India and many others, the U.S. continues to be one of the world's most cutting-edge places. The U.S. economy is huge, yet it continues to grow at a rapid pace, adding trillions of dollars in Gross Domestic Product over the past decade.

In this age of cut-throat global competitiveness, how can this be possible? After all, much of the economic news on television and in the newspapers is negative. We hear much about downsizing, off-shoring and diminishing U.S. economic clout. The U.S. population is growing, but at 300 million citizens, it's nothing compared to the billions that live in India and China. Our population comprises less than 5 percent of all people who live on the planet.

Given that, how can the U.S. continue to be such a dominant world force? Although the answer to this question probably has many components, one of the biggest reasons is creativity.

There's something about our system of government, our capitalist infrastructure and the American psyche that allows us to be innovators and discoverers. In a fast-moving, global, knowledge-based economy, the most innovative economy wins. Americans are creative. As a culture, it is one of our biggest strengths.

Just as nations live and die by their ability and willingness to be creative, so do individual people. If you want to be a successful professional, you must create.

The Hungarian-born, Nobel Prize-winning scientist Albert Szent-Gyorgyi once said, "Discovery consists of seeing what everybody has seen and thinking what nobody has thought."

Your creativity gives you security in an insecure, dynamic economy. You can't count on the same job being available for you for 30 or 40 years. Today's professionals must stand constantly ready to adapt to change. Creative thinking makes adaptation possible.

CREATIVITY IN SELF MARKETING

Just as creativity helps you survive in a dynamic economy, it is also critical to self marketing success. Creativity helps you stand out in a crowd. It makes you memorable, which is critical in the noisy marketplace. Creativity elevates you above your competitors and makes people remember you.

You can put your creativity to work as part of your self marketing efforts by doing something different. There is great power in being the first or only person to do something. There is also great power in creating something unique that is desirable to people. Do this enough and you will probably become very rich.

Successful people are always looking for unique ways to stand head and shoulders above the crowd. You could come up with new ideas to make money, to improve how your company does business, or innovative ways to market yourself. Regardless of the form in which your creativity manifests, it's a good idea to develop something valuable and attach your name to it.

When I worked as a college dean, I always looked for creativity as a personal trait when hiring directors and other professional staff members. The college where I worked had a reputation for being innovative, an important characteristic for a small private college trying to compete with much bigger institutions. Some of the creative things I developed while working in education administration not only helped the college, they boosted my career.

For instance, in the mid 1990s, the college was trying to boost enrollment in its undergraduate nursing program. At the time, we had excess classroom space. Meanwhile, the state of California was suffering from a shortage of nursing education programs.

To exploit the situation, we created a marketing campaign, targeting students at two-year colleges in California who were frustrated that they couldn't get into four-year colleges to finish their bachelor degrees. We designed promotional pieces, sent extensive mailings and purchased ads in junior college newspapers. I traveled to several California schools during this time and personally recruited prospective students.

The program was successful. In fact, the very first student who was admitted as a result of the program went on to be our student body president her senior year.

College recruiting, at least at that time, was very traditional and conservative. Every college did it the same way. The effectiveness of my outside-the-box model gave me confidence to try other innovative methods.

The college offered a master's degree program in nursing that was almost completely available via Internet and by using clinical proctors in the student's hometown. At the time, it was one of the few comprehensive, accredited distance learning programs in the field. To capitalize on this, we designed and implemented a unique program to recruit distance learning students from across the nation. The program's success led to an invitation for me to speak on my recruiting strategy at a conference in Memphis.

It matters not in which industry you work, you must be creative to stand out. Regardless of what your long-term career goals may be, creativity is an essential component of self marketing.

BECOMING MORE CREATIVE

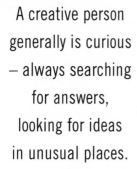

A creative person generally is curious – always searching for answers, looking for ideas in unusual places.

The playwright Edward Albee said, "The thing that makes a creative person is to be creative, and that's all there is to it."

Albee's statement is interesting. If I read it from one perspective, it appears to imply that you are either born with creativity or you are not. On the other hand, from a different perspective, he seems to be saying that a person can simply decide to be creative and thus enjoy a creative lifestyle.

I prefer the latter perspective on Albee's quote. Regardless of how creative you are today, you can become more creative tomorrow.

Experts claim that the average person loses a great deal of his or her creative-thinking abilities at age five, the start of kindergarten. The implication is that formal education stifles creative thinking. Regardless of whether this is true, children do appear to be more creative than adults. It doesn't have to be that way. Wherever you are in your career, you can recapture your youthful creativity again, but as an adult, you can harness it in a way that makes money and boosts your career.

A creative person generally is curious – always searching for answers, looking for ideas in unusual places. Creative types are well-rounded people and tend to be generalists instead of specialists. Leadership and creativity go hand-in-hand. Creative people aren't afraid to ask questions. In fact, they *enjoy* asking questions. As they hear answers to the questions, they are concocting ideas in their heads.

If you want to become more creative, strive to be more curious. Take some time out of your busy schedule each day and just learn. Go have lunch with someone who has absolutely nothing to do with your industry. Learn about your lunch partner's industry, life and goals. Ask lots of questions. Think about ways you can transpose this person's experiences into new ways to do your work better.

The legendary businessman Henry Ford once visited a beef-packing plant in Chicago. Ford took great interest in the way workers processed the beef from whole carcasses into small cuts of ready-to-sell meat. As he observed, it occurred to Ford that if the process was reversed, all the cuts would go back together to form a whole steer carcass again. The metaphorical light bulb switched on in Ford's head. "I can build automobiles this way," he thought. Ford went back home to Detroit and promptly created the famous assembly line.

You never know where inspiration will hit you. Not only should you be on the lookout for it, you must put yourself in a variety of places in hopes of finding it.

Creativity can come about by manipulating your existing knowledge and by drawing upon the things you have already experienced in life. In other words, creative people do not necessarily have to reinvent the wheel every day. The best ideas are borrowed and subsequently improved.

You can foster your creativity. I think of my best ideas when I'm taking long walks by myself. There's something about moving my body, watching the scenery and breathing fresh air that starts my mind twirling. Many people find inspiration in the shower – perhaps that explains why some people take so long in there.

Another way I foster creativity is to do mental exercises. I put a bunch of words in big letters on a piece of paper. The words relate to something I'm trying to accomplish personally or professionally. I stare at the words and just think about them. I let my mind wander. For some reason, new ideas just come to me when I do this.

Mind mapping is a good technique for developing ideas. You write a word that relates to the thing you are trying to accomplish. Then you think of other words that relate to the first word. Draw lines between the first word and the related words. Repeat the process for the related words. Before you know it, you'll have an entire sheet of paper full of words in circles connected to each other with a bunch of lines. This mental interconnectivity is a tremendous creativity facilitator.

I once attended a creativity workshop at a national conference in Kansas City. The speaker recommended we find new ideas from looking at existing things. The speaker referred to the technique as "forced relationships." Someone hoping to think of a new idea could select a topic and then randomly grab a few physical objects. Pondering the topic while thinking of ways that it related to the randomly chosen items can supposedly lead to new ideas.

AVOID THE ANTI-CREATIVITY TRAPS

Many normal human behaviors are anti-creative. As individuals and as a society, many of the things we value actually end up retarding our creativity.

For instance, we have a natural desire to administer things – to beat life into rational submission. We want to take ambiguous things and organize them. We like things to be logical and orderly. In reality, life is not administered in tidy little increments of rationality. It's messy. A tolerance for at least a little bit of messiness can boost your creative thinking.

Because we live in a complicated, technical world, we feel compelled to specialize. Jobs are often highly specialized. Colleges and universities make us choose majors. This often leads to advanced degrees, which burrow us further into the details of one narrow discipline. While this may bring us a high salary, it does not facilitate creative thinking. The most creative people tend to be generalists with a breadth of interests.

Laws, rules, policies and procedures play a big role in our lives. They are necessary in order to maintain a civil society. To be creative, however, you must sometimes bend the rules. History has shown that anytime people are oppressed by too many rules, innovation plummets.

It is natural to experience feelings of self-doubt, but too many people don't give themselves any credit for the creative abilities they already possess. Think back on your life to date. If you concentrate, I'm sure you will be able to identify a number of instances in which you were quite creative. Enjoy remembering your innovative success, and then tell yourself that you can be even more creative in the future.

Ambitious people can get so caught up in competing and achieving that they forget to reserve time for a little bit of fun. Professionals are under a great deal of pressure to produce. This can lead to feelings of guilt when you take time to play around. That's not healthy. Somehow, you must find time in your schedule for recreation and pure, carefree fun. Aside from the physical health benefits, recreation puts us in a frame of mind conducive to creative thinking.

During our school years, we were trained to search for absolute truths and identify the one best answer on tests. In life, however, there are more shades of gray than black-and-white truths. To be a creative person, you must know how to move back and forth between the shades-of-gray and black-and-white worlds.

If you are like most people, you hate making mistakes. Fear of failure may be preventing you from dreaming up an innovative idea and applying it. As long as you are striving to do something special, it is perfectly acceptable to fail. If you adopt such a philosophy, you're more likely to take on new risks. Without risk, there is no reward. Have courage!

GROUPTHINK

To foster creativity in any type of group – professional, social, political, for example – you must avoid the "groupthink" trap. Identified by sociologist Irving Janis, groupthink is a phenomenon attributed to the highly-cooperative atmosphere that can exist in the gatherings of self-confident experts.

Janis states that while high-cohesive groups are more effective than low-cohesive groups in achieving goals, some groups might be so closely bonded together that the problem-solving process, to which multiple minds must contribute, is disrupted, therefore producing undesirable solutions.

Janis was convinced that the concurrence-seeking tendency of close-knit groups can cause them to make inferior decisions. Since the atmosphere in such groups would be so strongly synergized, the individuals participating in these groups would be too receptive to other ideas and be wary of expressing their own ideas. This is due to the confidence level the individuals hold, and the respect they hold for each other.

In the business world, groupthink or similar phenomena happen regularly. Other negative behavior traits such as the herd mentality and fear of a charismatic leader can also stifle creativity. In order to have an innovative atmosphere in any organization, individuals must be empowered. Individualism must be respected.

Even if you work in a creativity-stifling environment, there are ways you can exercise your creative-thinking skills (especially outside of the office). If your workplace is oppressive, focus your creative skills outward. Doing so will be a pleasant distraction from the negative work environment. It could also lead you to new career opportunities.

Whether you are applying creativity to your work or to the ways in which you market yourself, it always pays to do something new in a way that others are not.

CHAPTER FOURTEEN

Never Stop Learning

AMERICANS ARE CURIOUS PEOPLE. WE LIKE TO EXPLORE. WE LIKE TO learn new things. This mentality goes back to the earliest days of our American culture.

The French scholar Alexis de Tocqueville observed this American trait during his landmark visit to the United States in 1831: "Born often under another sky, placed in the middle of an always moving scene, himself driven by the irresistible torrent which draws all about him, the American has no time to tie himself to anything, he grows accustomed only to change, and ends by regarding it as the natural state of man. He feels the need of it, more he loves it; for the instability; instead of meaning disaster to him, seems to give birth only to miracles all about him."

I love this quote, for it captures our spirit of intellectual curiosity and zealous pursuit of opportunity. I love the fact that this mentality was a part of America so long ago, and that, for the most part, it has remained a prominent part of our culture. From the early days, through the years and continuing in our modern time, Americans never stop learning.

It's a good thing, too, because that mentality is a major reason why our country has been so economically prosperous and competitive now despite the massive gains made by competing nations.

This macro view of America's intellectual curiosity applies to individual Americans as well. To come anywhere close to achieving the potential success that's inside you, you can never stop learning. Never!

LIFELONG EDUCATION

I have a side job as an adjunct faculty member at the University of Nebraska at Omaha where I teach an undergraduate course in real estate. I always teach in the spring semester, and typically about half of my students are in their final semester, about to graduate. I always chuckle to myself when I hear them say something like this: "I can't wait for graduation, so I never have to study again."

Not wanting to burst anyone's bubble, I say nothing, allowing them to enjoy the excitement of the approaching graduation. They'll discover soon enough that learning never ends.

High-achieving self marketers are students until they die or are so incapacitated they are no longer capable of doing anything. Let's focus for a moment on the "life" part of lifelong learning. You must pursue your curiosities until the end of your life. One might be tempted to think that learning can end with retirement, but that's short-sighted.

We're seeing a new trend – many successful professionals are choosing not to retire in the traditional sense. They may stop doing the high-stress, eight-to-five, daily job, but they keep working on their own terms. They may serve on boards, write articles, give speeches or work as consultants. One could make an argument that typical post-retirement work requires even more continuing education than the regular work a person did during a pre-retirement career.

The lifelong learning that successful self marketers must pursue is both formal and informal. If you have not yet finished a bachelor degree, it is worth your while to do so. If you have an undergraduate degree, you would probably benefit by pursing a graduate or professional degree.

If you are no longer interested in pursuing degrees, you will still find yourself in a classroom situation periodically. I enrolled in graduate school immediately upon receiving my undergraduate degree. I had a master's degree at a "traditional" age, my mid-twenties. Nevertheless, I still find myself in classrooms every now and then.

I sometimes take voluntary enrichment courses, often just one-day seminars, to learn something that will help me be more successful. When I wanted to enter the real estate field, I had to complete courses to be eligible to sit for the licensing exam. Now as an active licensee, I must take 12 hours of professional education courses every two years.

When I served as a dean at Clarkson College, I worked with many older, "non-traditional" students. I had great admiration for these students who, in their 40s or 50s, would resign from their current jobs only to return to college to study a completely different major.

High-achieving self marketers are students until they die or are so incapacitated they are no longer capable of doing anything.

Our largest major at Clarkson was nursing. We would have students enroll in our nursing program after working in a wide variety of business professions. I was always intrigued by the personal decision-making process that adult learners would go through when determining if they should leave their current career (and their regular salary), take out student loans and enroll in a health care education program.

Adult learners tend to be among the best students in any class. They've been through many battles in the real-world trenches. This experience gives them a different perspective than the traditional 20-year-old student brings to class. Many adult students would pursue their degrees while continuing to work fulltime. That's not easy, but it shows the dedication that is often necessary to achieve your career dreams.

TRANSFERABLE SKILLS

Among the hundreds of vocations in existence, nursing has traditionally been a "gateway job" that prepares its professionals for bigger and better things. In fact, few professions are as versatile as nursing when it comes to preparing people to take on completely different roles.

If you look around, you will find a large number of former nurses working in a variety of professional, management and executive jobs.

Why? First of all, nursing was traditionally one of the few professional jobs available for women. Many of the most talented and ambitious young women entered the nursing field. As more opportunities for women became available, there was a lot of latent management talent sitting in the nation's nursing ranks. When management and executive opportunities opened up to women, many ambitious nurses took the leap.

But there is an even better explanation of the disproportionate number of former nurses in big jobs: Nursing is a complicated field that demands its practitioners do a wide variety of activities. Nurses have highly developed logical-quantitative skills and must be outstanding communicators. They must be able to exhibit a great deal of compassion and empathy during stressful situations while working long shifts. After mastering all this, it is obvious why nurses become so successful in a number of professions.

Other professions like nursing give their professional members great transferable skills. If you are not thrilled with the work you are doing right now, think about the types of skills you have developed to date. How can these skills transfer to another profession? Are these skills marketable? What types of jobs would be well suited to your skill level?

If you determine you need additional skills to pursue a dream job, that's where lifelong learning comes in. Depending on what you're thinking about doing, you could take a couple courses, enroll in a new major or participate in short-term seminars.

Not every career change necessitates more formal training. You may simply need to read a few books or take on additional responsibilities at your current job. That could be all the additional education you would need.

PREPARING FOR OPPORTUNITIES

Lifelong learning can prepare you for unanticipated opportunities. Even if you are entirely satisfied with your current job, you need to be using your intellectual curiosity to further your career. By learning all you possibly can now, you will do a better job in your current job and set yourself up for future opportunities.

If you are an entrepreneur, continuing education will allow you to continually hone your craft. You will become better at operationalizing new innovations. You will be a better manager, more innovative and more likely to be on the cutting edge. You will also learn more effective ways to sell your products and services.

Lifelong learning allows you to prepare for a polarized reality of today's workplace. On one hand, you need to have a specialty – something that you do very well that few others can do. On the other hand, you need to be a generalist – someone with a diversity of professional skills and experiences. Shape your educational and intellectual pursuits in such a way as to pursue both of these seemingly dichotomous realities.

COMPETITION

Regardless of your line of work, it is healthy to assume that all your competitors are vigorously trying to improve themselves. You need to continue educating yourself just to stay up, let alone to get ahead.

Each of us is operating in a global, knowledge-based economy that is brutally competitive. Corporations are not the only entities that must fight competitors in every nation. Individual people do as well. To market yourself in our current economic environment, you must first develop an outstanding and diverse array of abilities.

Some self marketers are separating themselves from the pack by hiring life coaches or growth coaches. These are professionals who, for a fee, will coach you through your career like a basketball coach guides his players. Depending on the parameters of the coaching relationship, you will meet with your coach on a regular basis to review what you are doing professionally and to gauge how well you are doing it.

There is something almost magical about having another person to answer to. Essentially, that's what a coach is to you – someone who holds you psychologically accountable.

Many of the nation's top real estate salespeople hire sales coaches, with whom they meet on a regular basis. A very successful real estate agent whom I know spends $1,000 per month on her personal sales coach. She believes that the investment pays for itself many times over. She did well before hiring her coach but has been setting the world on fire since then.

This agent knows that, every week, she will have to answer to her coach. The coach can't do anything bad to her – he can't fire her. He can't punish her. He can, however, push her and ask her tough questions. Because she's paying so much for him, she WANTS to be responsive and accountable to him. She wants to please him by working hard and exceeding her personal goals.

If you don't have an extra grand to throw at a growth coach each month, you might be able to get a friend or trusted colleague to assume that role for free. You and a colleague can do each other a favor by being coaches to each other. It's a healthy, mutually beneficial relationship that could make both of you far more successful.

Getting a coach, whether a friend or a paid consultant, is yet another way to rise above the crowd. Although conceivably anyone could do this, only a small percentage of people will ever bother to go through the trouble of doing it. Taking a little time to better yourself and learn something new automatically puts you ahead of the vast majority of people.

SOFT SKILLS

When we think about improving ourselves, it's easy to think only about *formal* education, yet some of the best learning comes from *informal* education. You may assume that the most important things to learn are hard skills like accounting, law and a foreign language, but some of the biggest deficiencies among professionals are the so-called soft skills.

Soft skills are all those "other" things you need to master for success. Although they usually are not included in your written job description, soft skills determine whether you will be effective in carrying out your core responsibilities.

Knowing how to create a spreadsheet is a hard skill. Having the right attitude and mentality to learn new software is a soft skill. Knowing Generally Accepted Accounting Principles is a hard skill. A commitment to always being punctual is a soft skill.

Surprisingly, too many professionals, especially the younger or less experienced ones, have significant deficiencies in their soft-skill repertoires. Several surveys of business leaders have indicated great frustration about the sorry state of soft-skill competency among employees, even among professional employees.

A 2004 study conducted by Metropolitan Community College in Omaha indicated that employers would like to see better soft skills among employees in a few key areas: attendance and punctuality, customer service, desire to learn, teamwork, communication, follow through, professionalism, time management, problem solving, self initiative and organization.

Additional soft skills were mentioned less but still valued. These included perseverance, flexibility and a commitment to personal wellness.

Problem solving is a particularly valuable soft skill. Successful professionals develop a knack for identifying problems and developing solutions. The more efficient the solution, the more valuable you become as a professional.

Essentially, the subject of this book – self marketing – is a soft skill. Of course, it's a very important soft skill for your company and you personally. If you are an entrepreneur or high-ranking executive, your company depends on your self marketing abilities just to stay solvent. As an employee, you can use self marketing to help your company do more business.

The beautiful thing about soft skills is that you can further develop them by just practicing. Although there are classes to help you develop better people skills, leadership abilities and time management habits, you don't have to take these classes. You can improve by reading and just practicing soft skills in your current professional and community involvement activities.

NEGOTIATION AND PERSUASION

Your ability to negotiate favorable terms in a deal and to persuade others to your way of thinking is a tremendous asset. Professionals are well served to develop these skills continually. If you think about it, just about everything in your career is negotiable. You can never be too good as a negotiator.

Despite the importance of negotiation and persuasion skills, many professionals aren't all that great in these areas. It is well worth your time to study these skills and abilities and work to make yourself better. Classes, seminars and how-to books are helpful. After you know how to better negotiate and persuade, the next step is to practice, practice, practice.

Although negotiation is particularly important in the art of deal-making, persuasion is an everyday part of business life. Self marketers regularly find themselves in situations where they need to persuade others to their way of thinking. The art of persuasion is important whether you are trying to make a sale, a pitch in the boardroom or just convincing the boss.

A CHANGE OF SCENERY

Variety is a great pedagogical tool. To make sure you never stop learning, it's a good idea to deliberately change your point of view. You can do this by trying something new or going somewhere you have never been. Simple things like taking your work to the park with you or having quiet time alone to just think will give you a new perspective and put your mind in a better position to learn new things.

Travel is one of the best ways to open your mind to new discoveries. Every time I take a trip, whether for business or pleasure, I always come home with a new awakening. Spending time away from home, seeing different scenery and breaking up the monotony of your daily routine can be a real eye opener.

Just getting away from your office can be very helpful. That's why many companies take their staff members on retreats. Learning, thinking and discovery skills are sharpened when you get away from it all.

SET ASIDE TIME

Regardless of whether you need to improve your hard skills or your soft skills, lifelong learning should be an important part of your career. No matter how busy you get, you need to carve out time for this important self-development activity. Continuing education is like investing. Just as you should set aside investment money before you pay bills and pay for entertainment, you need to set aside time "off the top" for continuing education.

No matter how successful you become or how far in the career world you rise, you can always do more if you make a commitment to never stop learning.

From Ordinary to Extraordinary: Planning, Goal Setting and Time Management

UCCESSFUL PEOPLE ARE NOT AFRAID TO DREAM. THEY ARE VISIONARIES. Successful people transcribe their dreams and visions into clear, concise and quantifiable goals.

The most successful people have superior strategies for managing one of life's most precious resources: time. We can't control how many years we are privileged to live on this planet, but each of us receives 24 hours per day, 168 hours per week, and 8,760 hours per year.

Regardless of their chosen professions, good self marketers are focused on success. You need to have something about yourself that's extraordinary to be an effective self marketer. The only way you can become extraordinary is by mastering the principles of planning, discipline, goal setting and time management.

Planning is the process that maps out your journey from the present to a successful outcome in the future. You might accidentally be successful without planning, but it makes success much more likely. Nobody plans to fail, but too many people fail to plan. As legendary investor Warren Buffett said, "Someone is sitting in the shade today, because someone planted a tree a long time ago."

Discipline, or "personal motivation," is necessary because self marketing is a largely independent endeavor. The very term *self* marketing implies that it is something you do by yourself for yourself (although good self marketing also benefits any organization you are affiliated with). Even if you have a typical office job, you have to treat your self marketing work as its own business.

Personal motivation is critical if an entrepreneur is going to make a start-up business a success. The same holds true for self marketing. Self motivation is an internally generated force that directs you toward success and compels you to accomplish your goals. By focusing your mind and deliberately developing more successful life habits, you can intensify your personal motivation.

Some people appear to be born with more personal motivation than others. We can't control that. However, you can control how disciplined you are from this day forward.

In self marketing, personal motivation keeps you pushing forward even when you are discouraged, don't feel good or are too busy with more pressing matters. Because many of us have such busy schedules, it is tempting to make self marketing a low priority on our to-do lists. Self marketing is a prospecting opportunity. Whenever you have a huge deal to close, a job to interview for, or a crisis to solve, it is tempting to put prospecting activities on the back burner.

That's a mistake, because there is ALWAYS some crisis to deal with. Sure, you are going to spend more time in a given day on the hot issues, but some time should always be reserved for self marketing. It's kind of like saving a percentage of your income each week. You are tempted to spend it all on fun and frivolity now, and there are expensive pressing needs facing us all the time, but the responsible person saves a certain percentage of income each month before paying bills and buying entertainment. Self marketing is the same way – it needs to come off the top of your time balance sheet.

To insure that self marketing activities don't become permanently relegated to the back burner, you must be engaged in a personal planning process. This involves dreaming, visioning, goal setting and time management.

DREAMS

"We grow great by dreams," President Woodrow Wilson once said. "All big men are dreamers." I agree completely. It is highly unlikely that you will ever reach your success potential if you don't have some audacious dreams.

To start your journey toward better planning, start with dreams. Dreaming dreams is the highest, most important position on the planning-process hierarchy. Dreams can range from the reasonable to the outrageous and from practical to whimsical.

Each professional should sit down at least once every few years and just dream. Imagine what your ideal life looks like. Think about every single thing you would like to accomplish or experience in your life. A dream could be as far-fetched as traveling to the moon or as practical as getting rid of your credit card debt. All dreams are good dreams if they are your dreams.

Next, write your dreams on a piece of paper. Write down every single dream that enters your mind. Your list should be a stream of consciousness – the words originate in your head, travel through your arm, into your pen and onto the paper. Don't evaluate the practicality of the dreams and don't edit the wording – just get them on paper.

Don't worry if your list grows long. That's a good thing. After you have thought of every dream you can (don't be surprised if your dreams number in the hundreds), you may want to reorganize your dreams into categories. At this point it's okay to clean up your writing and edit the dream list as long as your editing doesn't change the meaning of your true desires.

CORE VALUES

After you have listed your dreams, it's time to work on your list of core values. These are the commitments that drive you each day. Core values indicate what is truly important to you. On a broad level, these values are related to your beliefs and philosophies of life. More narrowly, they relate to your behavior.

Core values are important to success, because they keep your inner self and your outward actions synergized. If you know where you stand philosophically and spiritually, you are more likely to make decisions in harmony with your true character. Acting this way will enhance your long-term career success and make you feel much better about the successes you achieve.

Perhaps your core values are integrity, ambition and respect for others. Who knows – you could have a long list of things you truly value. Regardless of what really matters to you, write your values on a separate piece of paper. Once you are finished, study your list of core values and think about why they are important to you.

By now, you will have accumulated a few pieces of paper. You'll need more for later steps in the planning process. Therefore, it's a good idea to start collecting all this information in a three-ring binder. Make a divider tab for each major portion of your personal planning process.

MISSION STATEMENT

After pondering your dreams and core values, it's time to work on your mission and vision. Dreams and values form the foundation of the mission and vision you have for your life and your career.

Mission can be defined as the basic purpose of your existence. You may decide to have a personal mission statement and a professional mission statement. Other people combine them into one. Your personal mission statement should be concise but still say a lot.

To formulate a personal mission statement, take a look at mission statements of companies and non-profit organizations. You can often find these on an organization's website or in the annual report. Notice what these organizations say in their mission statements and the format in which they are written. Adapt these examples to yourself. Write a mission statement as if you were an organization of one. After all, you are a business unto yourself.

Like the previous steps in this process, write your personal and professional mission statements on a piece of paper and add it to your personal planning process binder.

VISION

Highly successful people are visionary. This doesn't necessarily mean they are clairvoyant, but they can see opportunity in the future. Once you envision something, of course, you must work hard to make it come to fruition.

Vision is a snapshot of the future that compels you to move forward with purposeful confidence. Even though many people like to make vision statements complicated and full of flowery language, they should really be rather simple. As Yogi Berra said, "If you don't know where you're going, you might wind up someplace else."

Just like mission statements, most companies and organizations have vision statements. Look at them as samples and then craft a vision for yourself. Put the finished statement in your binder.

GOAL SETTING

The previous steps in the personal planning process will take a lot of time but will be quite beneficial for you. After going through all these laborious steps, you will have put yourself in the proper frame of mind to start setting your goals. Set goals that help you move closer to your dreams. Set goals that honor your core values and are in harmony with your mission and vision statements.

There are a number of reasons to set goals. They help you match actual with desired progress and give you a regular mile marker to chart your progress. Goals clarify and quantify your needs and wants.

It is wise to have short-, medium- and long-term goals. Long-term goals would be in the 10- to 20-year range. Medium-term goals are in the five-year range. Short-term goals are in the one-year range.

Goals are the bread-and-butter of your success plan. In my opinion, they are the most important part of your planning process. While the earlier steps can be conducted every few years, goals must be set yearly and evaluated at least monthly.

Each year, in November or December, all of the professionals in our company determine their goals for the coming year. Regardless of one's profession, experience level or current level of success, everyone should do this.

I started writing and tracking my goals in a very detailed manner the first year I was out of graduate school and into my professional career. I am so thankful I started this early in my adult life. Each year, there are very few goals that I do not accomplish. Everyone should be able to say this. If you follow the goal-setting and tracking process properly, it is an amazingly powerful career-success tool.

Simply setting goals in the first place is a great step; however, if you know how to manage the goal-setting process, you will be even more successful.

Goals should stretch you but still be within reason. The philosopher Ralph Waldo Emerson said, "We aim above the mark to hit the mark." You should set goals that will make you sweat a little bit but be realistically attainable.

There's a fine line between ambitious and unrealistic goals. "Setting goals for your game is an art," golfer Greg Norman said. "The trick is in setting them at the right level neither too high nor too low."

Next, make sure your goals are in writing. There is something very powerful about putting them in writing. Unwritten goals are no better than New Year's resolutions, and we all know how effective those are! Once your goals are on paper, you can't forget them. By putting them in writing, you are making a psychological commitment to yourself to pursue these goals. You have made yourself psychologically accountable, since your goals are now part of a permanent record.

To make yourself even more accountable, share your written goals with another person. By doing this, you remember in the back of your mind that another person knows what you stated you planned to do in the coming year. If you don't do it, that other person will know you failed. That alone is a powerful motivator.

The real estate agents in my office share their professional goals with the owner of the company and with me each year. Most of our people appreciate this, because it helps them do more deals and take home fatter checks. While we only ask them for their real-estate-related goals, some of the agents voluntarily give me their personal goals, just so they can be "accountable" to someone besides themselves. I find it flattering when they choose to be accountable to me, and I'm happy to serve in this role.

Choose the right person with whom you will share your goals. It should be someone you know and trust. It should be a person who can keep this personal information about yourself confidential and not judge you unfairly based upon your goals. Of course if some of your goals are exceedingly personal, you could keep them off the list that you share with the other person.

The more specific a goal is, the more likely you are to accomplish it. Goals should be quantitative or at least measurable. It is much better to state, "I will attend at least 20 networking events this year" instead of saying, "I will do a better job of networking." You can see that the first one is very clear. The second one is problematic, because it does not define or quantify "better." The goal, "I will reduce my body-fat index to 15 percent" is much better than "I will get in shape."

For annual goals, you may want to add a time element for further specificity. Examples might include: "I will eliminate 50 percent of my consumer debt by July 1." "I will earn a $20,000 bonus by the end of the first quarter." "I am going to give at least one presentation to a professional organization each month."

Because we live and work in a dynamic world, goals should be subject to change. Unforeseen circumstances or new priorities could arise during the year. There could be external circumstances beyond your control that suddenly shift your priorities. Perhaps you find out you are pregnant. Maybe you are fired from a job or offered a much better one. You could suffer the death of a loved one.

A myriad of happenings could force you to alter your goals. Don't change your goals at the drop of a hat, but if something truly important happens, don't be afraid to alter them.

GOAL TRACKING

Tracking is the magic ingredient that makes the goal-setting process so powerful. If you write your goals and put them in a binder that sits on the top shelf of a little-used cabinet, you are wasting a golden success opportunity.

Check your goals at least once a quarter, preferably once a month. As you read the goals, think about what you have and have not accomplished. Determine if you are on schedule. In other words, at the end of the first quarter, you should theoretically have accomplished 25 percent of your goals. At the end of the year, thoroughly review and evaluate your performance on each goal.

I have created a goal-tracking form that I use every year. I write each of my goals (both personal and professional) on paper. After each goal, I have a line for the date of completion. I also put in a line for writing notes or descriptive details. When a goal is completely accomplished, I place an "X" at the beginning of it.

Using a tracking form has done wonders for my career. Each year, my goal-tracking form is several pages long, yet I accomplish almost all of it. Any time I do anything related to one of my goals, I note it on my form. This is actually quite enjoyable for me. I derive great satisfaction anytime I cross off another goal.

I keep past years' goal-tracking forms for a record of my life. If I'm ever feeling down on myself or if self-doubt ever creeps into my mind, I can pull out last year's tracking form and remind myself that I have a lot to be proud of.

No matter how motivated you are and how diligent you are at tracking your goals, there is a good chance you won't accomplish 100 percent of your yearly goals. Don't beat yourself up too much if this happens. At the end of the year, simply evaluate why you didn't do it. Then determine if the unaccomplished goal still is consistent with your personal mission, vision and core values. If it is, move it to next year's goal-tracking form and get started on it earlier in the year. If the goal no longer is important to you, kill it and move on to more relevant goals.

TIME MANAGEMENT

In order to achieve your goals and become truly successful, you must develop superior time management skills. As the great management theorist Peter F. Drucker said, "Until we can manage time, we can manage nothing else."

If you need more investment capital, you can find it. If you need more talented people to work for you, you can find them. Unfortunately, you can never find more time. It is finite. It is fleeting in nature. Once it is gone, it can never be recovered.

Time is also a great equalizer – rich and poor, stupid and brilliant, everyone has the same number of hours in the day. Whether it's self marketing efforts or just life in general, the most successful people know how to manage their time effectively.

TIME WASTERS

Nobody actually perfects the art of time management. With dedication and practice, however, you can come close. The problem is that most people find time management to be very difficult. There are so many tempting time wasters in our lives. What's more, it's a heck of a lot more fun to sit around with friends, go out to dinner and watch television than it is to work efficiently.

Perhaps the most perilous time waster is television. According to the A.C. Nielsen Co., the average American watches more than four hours of television each day. For a little perspective, that's 28 hours per week, or even more disturbing, two months of nonstop television-watching per year. If the average American lives to be 80 years old, he or she would have wasted 13.3 YEARS OF LIFE watching television. What makes this statistic even more disturbing is that most of the stuff on television is low grade garbage.

Video games and Internet surfing are addictive for some people and become tremendous time wasters. Hobbies can become so consuming that the hobbyist's work and family life begins to suffer. Keep these fun activities in proper perspective.

In no way am I saying that in order to be more successful, you have to extinguish all fun from your life. That would be terrible. Fun-haters don't live as long as the typical person and their lives are not as meaningful. Just be careful to schedule your fun and manage how much of your time is spent on it. You need recreation in life, but if you have ambitious goals, you simply won't be able to slack off as often as some of your buddies. To be more successful, you will need to make some sacrifices.

When you do schedule fun and free time, try to focus on something that's healthy for both mind and body. For instance, physical activities or mentally interactive activities are better for you than a mindless, passive activity like watching television.

Other time wasters include too much socializing, being constantly interrupted, procrastination, disorganization, perfectionism, lack of planning, fear of failure and the inability to say "no."

TIME MANAGEMENT SECRETS

Although time management is never easy, there are a number of things you can do to make yourself better at it.

Organize Your Life

This is easier to say than to do but, above all, make a commitment to being punctual. Running late is a huge time waster. You often have to make up excuses to explain your tardiness. You end up going through extra steps because you weren't punctual. If you are the boss, your tardiness affects your workers, which ultimately costs you money in lost productivity. If you are a perpetually late person, make a commitment to leave a little earlier than you normally do. The peace of mind you get from not having to rush from one place to another makes that extra effort all worth it.

If you have a hard time getting work done punctually, set deadlines. Many people can't complete projects unless they impose deadlines on themselves. If you want to undertake some self-marketing activities to improve your career, deadlines are very important. That's because for most people, self marketing activities are additional or external to their jobs. In your regular work duties, you have a boss to answer to. In your self marketing efforts, you answer only to yourself.

Always think about how the tasks you do each day relate to your goals. Ask yourself, "Are the ways I choose to spend my time directly helping me achieve my goals and therefore moving me closer to realizing my dreams?" If the answer is "no," you are not organizing your life properly.

> **Time is also a great equalizer – rich and poor, stupid and brilliant, everyone has the same number of hours in the day.**

Organizing your life is necessary to operationalize your goals. Break your goals into smaller objectives and tasks. It's much easier to tackle your goals if the actual work is broken into time increments of 30 minutes or less.

You need to have some sort of calendar tool such as an appointment book, a program on your computer, a Personal Data Assistant (PDA) or a more advanced device like a Blackberry. If you are still at the paper calendar and address book level, consider going electronic; it's much more efficient. If you are at the PDA level, consider upgrading to a higher technological standard. There is great time-management technology out there. If better technology will make you more efficient, you would be foolish not to use it.

I recommend making a daily, or at least weekly, to-do list. This can be on paper, or it can be integrated into your PDA or other time management technology. Although I have Outlook on my computer and a Palm Treo as my phone/PDA, I still make my to-do lists on paper. The reason for this is I love the psychological pay-off I get every time I make a line slashing through another item on the list. Crossing off completed work from the list simply feels good.

Be Efficient

Efficiency in time management requires that you avoid doing anything unnecessary. Notice how many steps it takes you to complete a task. Are there unnecessary steps? If so, cut them out and save yourself time.

Do each task only once. It is often tempting to start something then back away from it. When you return to the task, you have to "catch up" to where you left off. For some reason, a lot of professionals will repeat their efforts on a given task. This makes no sense.

Similarly, you need to be very efficient with papers and emails. Sometimes I will catch myself being horribly inefficient as I'm going through my paper mail. I'll pick up a bill, glance at it and decide I want to deal with it later. I'll see a trade journal, glance at an article, then decide to read it more carefully some time later when it is quiet, and I can concentrate more. Behaving this way is a mistake.

Pick up a piece of paper only once. As you have it in your hand, you must make a quick decision. You will act on it, file it, or throw it away. Try not to set it back on your desk after you pick it up. This will only cause you to waste time looking at it again.

Treat emails the same way. A cluttered in-box is a sign of bad time management. When an email comes in, act on it and then file it in a folder or delete it. Leaving your in-box full of partially read emails shows a deficiency in your professionalism. Be wary of all the jokes, political or human-interest emails that your friends and family send to you. I get scores of these every day. If I read every one of these personal emails, I would never get anything done. You can waste a big part of your day reading emailed fluff. When it comes to email, be decisive!

Another way to enhance your efficiency is to make good use of transit time. Always bring some work with you in case you find yourself sitting in a waiting room before an appointment. If you have five minutes, whip out your laptop or some notepaper and get to work. Use every little nook and cranny of time you can find.

It also makes sense to use transit time for making phone calls. As long as you are careful and it is legal in your state, you can use drive time to catch up with calls. Working in commercial real estate, I spend part of my day driving around to properties and going to meetings. I use this time to return calls.

First Things First

I admit it: I'm a born procrastinator. It's part of my DNA. I have to fight it constantly. When I was in college, I could put off writing a paper or studying for a test with amazing creativity. The closer the test came, the more I'd feel like cleaning the apartment, vacuuming my car or doing my laundry – anything but the thing I really should have been doing.

I'm glad my job requires me to commute to an office building. I don't think I could work effectively at home. There have been a couple of times over the years when circumstances dictated that I had to work a day from home. For a procrastinator, that's hard. I'd work for a little while and then decide the house needed to be picked up. I'd work for a half hour and then realize I was hungry again. I must have made 10 trips to the refrigerator the last time I "worked from home."

Procrastinators must learn to put first things first. Beating procrastination isn't easy, but it helps if you force yourself to do the most important thing first. Good time management requires that you prioritize your work. Determine what is most important and do it first. Just get it done. Then go on to the second most important thing. Avoid the temptation to quickly do the fifth most important thing right away just because it's easy and won't take a lot of time. Stick to your priority order, and you will go a long way toward beating the disease of procrastination.

Frequently ask yourself, "What's the best use of my time right now?" If you are not doing that, you are not following your priorities and are thus wasting time. As you become more successful, you will want to spend your precious time pursuing the activities that you enjoy the most and give you the highest monetary return. The other activities should be hired out or delegated to a subordinate. Doing too many routine, minor things keeps you from accomplishing something great.

Perfectionism Is a Trap

While it would be really nice to be perfect, it's a waste of effort. Absolute perfection is impossible for imperfect beings like us who live in an imperfect world. We can strive to get as close as possible, but that's as good as it gets.

An obsession with the elusive idea of perfection is truly one of the biggest time wasters in human history. Perfectionists often turn into procrastinators. The problem is that you are likely not to start an endeavor until you are convinced that you can be perfect at it. That never happens, so you keep putting it off.

The great military general George S. Patton said, "A good plan, violently executed now, is better than a perfect plan next week." Patton knew that obsessing about perfection would lead to indecision and inactivity. In war, that causes defeat.

Perfectionism can lead to paralysis. If you desire perfection so badly, you may also develop a great fear of failure, the opposite of perfection. The world's most successful people are risk takers; they never allow fear of failure to keep them from making things happen.

Don't Stand in Temptation's Way

As mentioned earlier, some of the biggest time wasters are television, video games and excessive web surfing. One of the best ways you can avoid these and other time wasters is to remove yourself from tempting situations.

For instance, my wife and I recently purchased a large armoire for the television on the main floor of our house. When we're not deliberately watching something, we close the doors of the armoire. That alone makes it less tempting to waste time watching television, because we can't actually see the television.

If you feel as if you spend too much time playing games and surfing online, turn your computer all the way off, go outside and do some physical activity. Eventually, this will help you moderate your use.

Watch out that you don't get too involved in hobbies or that "extracurricular" things start to become more important than your real job or your family. Hobbies and other forms of involvement are very healthy, but you have to treat them like alcohol – too much of a good thing is actually a bad thing.

Speaking of alcohol, studiously avoid addictive activities. People who excessively smoke, drink, gamble or do illegal drugs typically waste tremendous amounts of precious time and are significantly less successful.

Although it is tempting to micromanage people and projects, don't allow yourself to get too involved in unnecessary details. Sure, you need to make sure YOUR details are taken care of, but you don't need to get involved in someone else's.

Gossip is a colossal time waster. It is also one of the most tempting ways to waste time. Gossip can drive a stake into the heart of any organization. It can become an insidious force that has destroyed many organizations and careers. When people gossip, they exert tremendous energy and mental focus toward a harmful activity. It is an amazingly negative phenomenon that unfortunately seems to pervade humanity.

Not only do gossip sessions hurt people, they can chew up hours of clock time. You have to be careful, because often gossipers start talking about someone under the guise of "fixing a problem" or "making you aware of something." Watch out as soon as the conversation starts bashing on people. The best thing to do is end that conversation immediately. Get up and walk out, change the subject or just say you don't want to talk about anyone in a negative tone. That will usually shut up the gossiper right away.

When you dislike someone, it's very tempting to jump into the black hole of gossip. Avoid it. You will only lessen your professional image and take time away from much more valuable endeavors.

Plan Ahead

Thousands of years ago, Plato said, "The beginning is the most important part of the work." While you don't want to over plan, you would be wise to set aside a small amount of time each morning, to plan and organize your day. This will increase your efficiency, allowing you to accomplish much more in the same amount of time. Generally speaking, time spent planning is time well spent.

Interruptions

Among the most frustrating time wasters are interruptions – unplanned visitors, spontaneous conversation and water-cooler talkers. Some interruptions are maddening; others are completely legitimate but still make it hard to focus.

Each interruption causes you to stop what you are doing. You then spend time talking to the person who interrupted you. Almost every conversation you have as a result of an interruption usually lasts longer than is really necessary. When you are finally done with the interruption, you have to relocate where you stopped working and remember what exactly you were doing. That takes time.

There are a number of ways you can reduce the intrusiveness of interruptions or even eliminate them altogether.

First of all, just because your phone rings doesn't mean you have to answer it. Just because you just received a new email in your inbox doesn't mean you have to read it right now. Just because someone knocks on your door doesn't mean you have to answer it. In other words, it is sometimes wise to put off these small annoyances until you get your meaningful work done. Later, you can go back and answer all emails and return all voice mails at one time.

When I am running late or am busy doing errands around town, it seems like I inevitably run into someone I know. Anytime you bump into an acquaintance in a random public place, there is this unwritten rule that forces you to spend a couple minutes chatting. When you're terribly busy, you can't afford to do this. Want a way out of it? Wave at the person from a distance, shout "hi" and then mumble something about being late as you keep walking. It works like a charm.

Also effective is the "stand-up technique." If an interrupter walks into your office or cube, stand up to talk to them. This gives the interrupter a non-verbal cue that you are not able to sit around and shoot the breeze. If your interrupter doesn't catch on, walk slowly toward him. He will instinctively drift backwards. Keep doing this until you have gently pushed him to your door or the opening of your cube. Usually, the person will leave and not even realize that you facilitated his rapid departure. This is a great way to end an interruption without hurting anyone's feelings.

If you have pressing work you must complete, you may want to consider declaring "do-not-disturb time." Tell your colleagues that you are doing something important and that for a certain amount of time, nobody should disturb you unless it's a true emergency.

One of the commercial real estate agents in my firm is highly effective using the telephone to prospect for clients. He sets aside two hours in the morning and two hours in the afternoon as his designated calling time. The secretaries and his fellow agents know not to bother him during these times. During the rest of the day, when he works with colleagues, meets with clients, works on contracts, etc., he is much more open to being interrupted.

If you have an office, sometimes you should just close the door. You don't want to do this too often or you run the risk of being perceived as distant, exclusive and unhelpful. If you don't have a private office at work, you may want to see if you can periodically borrow a conference room or another quiet place when you have work that requires heavy concentration and no interruptions.

Unfortunately, some people are just so damned clueless, they'll interrupt you anytime and anywhere. To these people you sometimes have to be bold and just cut them off.

The Meeting Trap

Comedian Fred Allen once quipped, "A committee is a group of men who individually can do nothing but as a group decide that nothing can be done."

Few things cause professionals to roll their eyes in disgust more than a disorganized, unnecessary meeting. In today's business world, there are simply too many meetings. The majority of meetings we go to are unnecessary. Even if a meeting is needed, the majority of time during the meeting is filled with unnecessary content.

The first tip on dealing with meetings is to avoid them. If you are in charge, try to find ways that your people can be empowered to make individual decisions at the lowest possible level. Good organizations should expect professional team members to keep each other informed, but, for the most part, they should be encouraged to behave as confident individuals.

> Success in business is measured by power, influence and money, not by the number of meetings you attend each week.

If your presence is not absolutely essential, try to get out of going. Don't go to meetings just for the sake of making your calendar look more impressive. If you don't have an active role in the meeting, and assuming your boss isn't ordering you to attend, try to get out of it. Success in business is measured by power, influence and money, not by the number of meetings you attend each week.

If you have to go, there are ways of making it more efficient. If you are in charge of the meeting, create an agenda in advance. Stick to the agenda and don't allow people to stray far from it. Use good meeting facilitation techniques to keep it moving. You will have to periodically bring people back when they go off on verbal tangents.

When I must attend a meeting in which I do not have a very active role, I bring paperwork with me. I sit in the corner or end of the room and do my paperwork while the meeting is going on. If you do this discreetly, most people won't mind, and you'll get some work done. This was an especially valuable practice when I was a college dean. Academic institutions are famous for holding too many unnecessary meetings. The college I worked for was no exception. Over the years, I was able to get a great deal of work done while sitting in five or six hours of meetings each day.

Be Realistic

I tend to be too ambitious when I plan out my day. For some reason, I always think I can do more than I really can in the time allowed.

I'm one of those guys who looks at the clock on a Saturday evening and see that I have one hour before my wife and I have to be at a dinner party. Sure enough, I'll convince myself that I can reorganize the basement, pull weeds from the lawn plus shower and get dressed in that short period of time. Experience tells me that this is not realistic, but for some reason I try to pull it off.

Don't fall into that trap. Be realistic with your time. Trying to do too much in a short time frame causes too much stress and leaves unfinished projects dangling.

Remember, you can't work all the time. No matter how ambitious you are, you need some sleep, and you need to reserve some time for fun.

Just Say No

The better you are as a self marketer, the more people will want you to join their committees, political groups and service clubs. For example, I give a lot of speeches to various groups. Almost all of them ask me to join.

The more successes you enjoy, the more boards and charity organizations are going to try to draft your talent for their causes. This is all quite flattering, but there are limits to what you can handle. Don't do so much volunteer work (even if it is good self marketing) that you end up getting fired from your real job and divorced from your spouse.

There have been times when I allowed myself to get way too busy. In the months leading up to the birth of my son, I resigned from seven organizations. Despite this, I still was involved in five major activities in addition to my main job as a commercial real estate professional.

If you can't handle any more, you will find great liberation in saying "no." Just say it as politely and respectfully as you can, so you don't burn a bridge you may need to cross again in the future.

Focus

You will pay dearly in the currency of wasted time if you don't focus. Although you may have an overwhelming amount to do, concentrate on one thing at a time. This will keep you from going loony. Don't jump from one thing to another haphazardly. Try to finish or at least come to a logical stopping point before shifting your attention elsewhere.

If someone else is giving you instructions, listen carefully the first time. If you have to go back to have information repeated, you are wasting sweet time.

Once you have a plan for your career success and how you're going to market yourself, try to stick to it unless you are convinced it is not working. Avoid constantly shifting your priorities. Deviate from your carefully developed success plan only for legitimately important reasons.

Reserved Personal Time

On the face of things, personal time might seem like a waste. After all, when you're relaxing, you're not making progress toward your goal of world domination or whatever it is that you wish to accomplish. Nevertheless, your long-term success is enhanced when you take time to exercise, eat properly and get a full night's sleep.

Having a strong relationship with your significant other will make you feel better about yourself and your life. Therefore, time spent with your special someone as well as family and friends is a great investment. It recharges your emotional battery and reminds you why you are working so hard.

High achieving people reserve "thinking time" for themselves. Periodically, go to a quiet place where you are unlikely to be interrupted. Just let your mind wander. When I do this, I am always amazed at the great ideas that seemingly just pop into my head.

If you enjoy quality personal time, you will have a better sense of when your physical and mental peak times of the day and week occur. Use this knowledge to your advantage. Save your most intellectually challenging work for the times when you are at your daily mental peak.

Avoid Duplication

Delegate, delegate, delegate! That is one of the best things for a manager to remember. For many managers, it is difficult. Anytime we delegate, we are giving up some of our control. If you do not delegate, however, you will probably burn yourself out. Nobody can be a high-functioning professional and an effective self marketer without delegating the little stuff to someone else.

We also suffer from needless duplication when we try to reinvent the wheel. The best ideas are borrowed and then adapted to your needs. Why try to reinvent something that already exists and is readily available to you?

Staying organized and keeping track of your information helps you manage your time. If you lose an important piece of paper, you could spend hours looking for it, or if you never find it, recreating it. Having and following a good system of organization will save you copious amounts of lost time.

Finally, technological devices allow us to avoid duplication by making things much faster. If you are not taking advantage of the many technologies that are making us more effective while bolstering our free time, you are essentially duplicating your efforts.

Take Control

Ultimately, no one but you should be able to control your time and how you use it. If you allow people to abuse your time, they will happily do it. People tend to be rude and obnoxious when it comes to time usurping.

President Lyndon B. Johnson once said, "Heck, by the time a man scratches his behind, clears his throat and tells me how smart he is, we've already wasted 15 minutes."

Decide that you are in control of your time and don't let others take over. Cut people off if you have to or at least steer them away, so they don't suck your time away.

It pays to really know who you are and what your real strengths are. Whatever you determine, exploit your strengths and prioritize your time.

Finally, you will make a positive impression and build rapport with another person if you are respectful of his or her time. Try not to interrupt needlessly. Be punctual to meetings. Showing respect for another person's time is a productive way to network and build a group of allies.

CHAPTER SIXTEEN

Make It Look Easy: Perpetual Professionalism

S HOTS RANG OUT IN WASHINGTON, D.C., AT 2:27 P.M. ON MARCH 30, 1981, as John Hinckley attempted to assassinate President Ronald Reagan outside the Hilton Hotel. Within seconds, the presidential motorcade was rushing toward George Washington University Hospital's emergency room.

Despite coughing up blood and laboring to breathe, the President refused when a Secret Service agent offered to help him out of the limousine. Under his own power, Reagan stood up tall and strong, straightened his tie and walked to the emergency room door with the distinguished dignity we expect from the President of the United States.

He collapsed as soon as he reached the door and soon lost consciousness. Although he nearly died that day, Reagan insisted on maintaining his professional image to the best of his ability even in his most dire moment. Always dapper, always a gentleman, Reagan knew that professionalism was a critical part of his long and successful career.

Most of us will never be expected to maintain a professional image in the face of an assassination attempt, but Reagan's behavior that awful day is a model for all of us. Highly successful people value professionalism. They strive to exhibit professional behavior at all times.

MAKE IT LOOK EASY

The best self marketers just seem to ooze success. It pours out of their very being kind of the way charisma seems to pour out of exceptionally popular people. The aura of success and professional image go hand-in-hand, feeding off each other and building upon one another.

For some lucky people, this ability appears to come naturally. Others have to work at it. Regardless, anyone can enhance his or her professional persona through deliberate effort.

Perpetual professionalism in self-marketing means you market yourself without making it *look* like you are marketing yourself. Self marketing should become second nature to you, something that you do almost automatically. This can happen if you consciously strive to ingrain good habits into your very being. Consistency is critical.

Any time you meet someone, make sure to smile and use the person's first name. Commit that name to memory and use it every time you see that person. Always look people in the eye and give them an enthusiastic and firm-but-not-bone-crushing handshake. These behaviors are foundational. They are minimum expectations of good self marketing, but, surprisingly, many people do not exhibit them.

DRESS CODE

As a professional, your dress and appearance should be first rate. Out of respect for the office, some U.S. Presidents have said they never took off their suit jackets when they were in the Oval Office, even when working late at night.

In most cities over the past 10 to 15 years, professional dress standards have taken a nose dive. Professional dress has become extremely casual. In some ways this may be a good trend: It costs less to dress casually and feels much more comfortable. I'm afraid, however, that the casual work environment has gone too far.

Those who dress too casually run the risk of being taken lightly by their colleagues and clients. I'm rather conservative when it comes to dress, so I have always valued professional attire. I'm a big believer that savvy professionals dress for the career level they hope to attain someday instead of the one they occupy right now.

That's why I wear a suit most days unless the weather is exceptionally bad or I have absolutely nothing going on. You have to be careful, however, when you assume nothing important is going on in a given workday. It must be a Murphy's Law thing, but it seems like unexpected meetings always pop up on a day I dress down. As soon as I show up for work without a tie, a prospective client stops by.

When you are the only person at an event not dressed professionally, you will probably feel self-conscious. You may not be taken as seriously as your better-dressed counterparts especially if you are young or have youthful looks.

Professionals who work for Internet companies or other famously casual employers would feel out of place wearing a suit to work. That's fine, but casual-company employees should have some business clothes always ready in case they are invited to a dress-up event. You don't want to miss an opportunity, just because you don't have time to switch out of your flip-flops and t-shirt.

Like your clothing, your accessories should convey a sense of professionalism. Women tend to have more accessories than men, so this is of greater concern to the ladies. That said, men and women carry notebooks, briefcases, laptop computer bags and business card holders, for example. Any accessory should be in good, clean condition and not look cheap.

Be careful not to overdo it with cologne and perfume. Less is more. Few things are more annoying than standing in an elevator with some guy who reeks like the department store cologne counter. Professional workplaces are not meat markets. You are not there to give off pheromones to the opposite sex. You are there to make money and advance your career.

STICKING YOUR NECK OUT

Professionals who are striving to establish name recognition and positive public images have to stick their necks out. People will watch your every move and judge your every action. What's more, you can never be sure who is watching and when they are watching. That's why savvy self marketers assume they are always on stage and behave accordingly.

As a self-marketing professional, you are like an actor on stage – you must never fall out of character.

As a self-marketing professional, you are like an actor on stage – you must never fall out of character. If you do, your personal "audience" will pick it up in a heartbeat. You are also like a politician. Instead of running for a government office, however, you are running for a personal "election." You need to project the right image to your "voters" (your personal target audience) upon whom you depend for support.

When you assume you're being watched, you're more likely to be more conscientious and avoid doing things that hurt your image. Never engage in personal hygiene activities in public. When you go to a client's office, never park in the front row. Be considerate and save the best parking stall for your client's clients.

When you stick your professional neck out and become a public figure, you have to make some sacrifices. As you become more successful, no matter how well you treat people, some will become jealous of you. It's human nature to resent those who are more accomplished. It's one of the negative byproducts of success. Don't give a jealous person any ammunition. You just can't behave recklessly in public, because someone can and will use it against you.

PRIVATE VS. PROFESSIONAL LIVES

Some of the most clean-cut, buttoned-down people at work can be downright wild in their personal lives. That's fine as long as it doesn't interfere with your work. As an old boss of mine used to say, "If you're going to hoot with the owls tonight, you better be ready to soar with the eagles tomorrow morning." Don't let your off-duty antics ruin your effectiveness on the job.

Typically, people are much more apt to make reckless decisions in their personal lives than in their professional circles. The problem is that many of your personal choices can end up having a detrimental effect on your professional life.

For instance, many companies do background checks on employees. I never hire anyone without doing a background check, searching their criminal history and motor-vehicle record. If the job has financial responsibilities, I look at the candidate's credit report.

In addition to the formal background check, I like to Google prospective employees. Many employers do this. You can find out an amazing amount of information about someone with a simple search. People are Googling their dates before going out with them, so it seems only logical that employers would Google would-be employees. I try to find anything online that I should know before making a decision. If you develop a questionable track record, it will likely show up during the background check and Internet search.

> What's done in the name of fun can sometimes make you look quite unsuitable to a prospective boss or client.

Along these same lines, employers are signing up for MySpace.com and FaceBook.com just so they can search for prospective employees' profiles. If you have ever visited one of these social networking sites, you know that many of the profile pages are full of party pictures and sexual innuendos. Your prospective boss doesn't want to see your Cancun vacation photos and a beer bottle in your hand. What's done in the name of fun can sometimes make you look quite unsuitable to a prospective boss or client.

If you are making a commitment to market and promote your personal brand, it's time to ditch the juvenile email addresses. If you have a silly, obnoxious or sexually suggestive email address, keep it among your friends. Nobody wants to do business with "*rugbydude@hotmail.com.*" Nobody wants to hire "*sexkitten@hotmail.com*" – at least not for legitimate, professional purposes. I am amazed at the ridiculous email addresses people will list on their resumés.

Similarly, you should avoid cutesy announcements on your voice mail. Once you give out your home or cell phone number to a business-oriented contact, that line is no longer personal. Make sure your recorded announcement is professional. It may be cute to have your three-year-old record the message, but that doesn't really play well when a busy executive calls to set up an interview. You may think it's cool to record your announcement over music in the background – it's not. To someone calling you on business, it's annoying. Also, avoid the rude, curt announcements like "you know what to do at the beep." You should keep your recording concise while speaking in a pleasant, professional voice.

PROFESSIONAL COMMUNICATION

To be perpetually professional, you must have good communication habits. Whether it's written, visual or verbal communication, you must be skillful.

First of all, use proper grammar in your writing. Grammatical errors really stand out on a written page. Using poor English in your speaking diminishes your image too. Make sure you brush up on the little things like using adjectives and adverbs properly. Practice speaking with logical, well-structured sentences.

Email is one of the greatest business tools ever invented. It has increased productivity and lowered communication costs exponentially. Text messaging is also an efficient tool. Unfortunately, these technologies have given too many people excuses for being poor writers.

Too many professionals write business correspondence the way they email their closest friends: "How R U? 2 cool seeing U @ the party! – i up 2 L8 last nite! – LOL." While this may make complete sense to a lot of Americans, especially those in generations Y and X, it's a foreign language to many others. Even if a colleague understands "Emailese," don't use it in professional communication. In the business world, writing should be professional. Your reputation depends on it.

The mobile telephone is another business technology that has revolutionized productivity. I spend so much time talking on mine, I often wonder how I ever managed to do deals before they existed. But with the cell phone revolution has come one of the biggest mistakes a business person can make – rudely interrupting a face-to-face business meeting to take another call.

Do not (I repeat: do not) take cell phone calls when you are meeting in person with a colleague and especially with a client. This is one of the rudest things business people do today. If you do this, you are telling the person with whom you are meeting that they are not important and that they can be set aside while you do business with someone who is more valuable.

You may think that taking calls at any time makes you more efficient. This is actually a fallacy. Every time you take a cell phone call during a meeting, you have to pause, offering an insincere apology for your intention to take a call. Then you speak on the phone. Because there is someone sitting across the table staring at you, you will probably not be at total liberty to say all that you would if the conversation was more private, which means you'll be calling the person a second time after the meeting.

When you finally hang up the phone, you then take time to apologize for the interruption. Then it takes time to catch back up to where you were in your first conversation. Meanwhile, the momentum and flow of your meeting has been compromised. This is inefficient and ends up costing you more time in the long run.

Even worse, answering a cell phone is incredibly inconsiderate of the other person. Everyone is busy – not just you. For every minute that your meeting counterpart has to sit staring at you conversing with someone you perceive to be more important, he or she becomes restless, irritated and resentful of you.

If you truly want to make an impression in your networking meetings with people, turn that damned phone off until the meeting is done.

WRITTEN MATERIALS

Self marketers carry with them a supply of printed support materials. Never go to a meeting without an ample supply of business cards. If you are a new entrepreneur or if your employer doesn't provide you with cards, wait no longer. Go to the office supply store. Buy some business card stock. Design your cards and print them right away.

Give your business card to everyone you meet in any business setting. To be safe, keep a supply in your wallet, purse, suit jacket, portfolio, briefcase, home, car, everywhere.

In certain circumstances, you need something more in-depth than a business card. Every professional should have a one-page bio with a picture included. It's like a fancier version of a resumé, designed for prospective clients or other VIPs with whom you may interact. Clients want to know about the people they may be engaging for professional services. Have both a printed and electronic version of an executive bio-with-picture ready to go at a moment's notice.

Make sure your resumé is always polished and ready to be distributed at any time. Perhaps your current job has you happier than a pig in mud. Perhaps you are a business owner who couldn't fathom the thought of working for someone else again. It doesn't matter. You need a professional resumé for unsolicited opportunities that could come your way.

Even if you are not looking for a job, your dream job may present itself at any time. Likewise, an exciting part-time, side job may become available, requiring you to submit a resumé. For a variety of reasons, perpetually professional self marketers have the resumé ready to be fired off at any moment.

By the way, resumés and executive bios should be printed on quality paper using a high-quality printer. Of course, you will probably distribute most of your bios/resumés electronically. That's why you should turn your resumé into an Adobe PDF. It's unprofessional to send a resumé in a format where people can make changes to it.

A WORLDLY PERSPECTIVE

You will come across far more professionally if you know what's going on outside your immediate sphere of interest. True professionals keep up with current events in the world and inside their industries.

To keep up with the happenings in your area of expertise, subscribe to professional journals and trade magazines. As a commercial real estate agent, I read *Midwest Real Estate News, National Real Estate Investor, Heartland Real Estate Business* and *Midlands Business Journal*. Most industries have their own publications.

Conventions and seminars are effective ways to keep up with the industry. Large professional associations tend to hold state, regional and national conventions. These events have the added benefit of being great networking opportunities.

Few things are as unimpressive as a management-level person who doesn't know what's going on in the world. When sitting around a table with a group of other professionals, you should be able to keep up with any conversation. If the discussion shifts to politics, you are expected to know what's going on in the world. Your colleagues will lose respect for you if you are obviously naïve about the happenings in the world.

In addition to keeping up with national and world news, keep an eye on local affairs. Many businesses are tied closely to the cities where they do business. You should be up on the major business, political, cultural and social aspects of your city.

PLAY NICE WITH OTHERS

True professionals are empathetic. They seek to understand others and treat them with respect. Whether you perceive a person to be above you or below you on the socioeconomic food chain, treat every-one with respect. Aside from being the right thing to do, this will

Whether you perceive a person to be above you or below you on the socioeconomic food chain, treat everyone with respect.

endear you to those you meet and make them like you. In self marketing, it doesn't get better than that.

One way to respect others is to honor their time. Be punctual to meetings. It is inconsiderate to keep people waiting. If something comes up preventing you from being on time, call the person's cell phone and let them know. Everyone is busy. I certainly appreciate people who are considerate of my time.

You can honor someone else's time by being efficient in your dealings with them. Try hard not to make anyone duplicate the efforts they undertake on your behalf. Communicate clearly to avoid wasteful ambiguity. If you call a meeting, make an agenda and deliberately keep the meeting moving along, preferably ahead of schedule.

Sometimes it is hard to return calls promptly especially when your voice mail is inundated. Common courtesy demands that we return a call as soon as possible and no longer than 24 hours after the message is recorded. To lessen burdens on their schedules, many people return calls while traveling or waiting for a meeting to start.

Finally, some people tend to show respect to high-ranking people, while disregarding their run-of-the-mill colleagues. This is dangerous, because someone who is leading a seemingly unremarkable career could become a powerful decision-maker at a later date. Sure, it's a good idea to focus most of your self marketing efforts on people who can do something for you now, but don't forget to foster other relationships that could bear fruit years down the road.

TAKE CONTROL

No one can force you to become perpetually professional. It's a commitment that must come from your own mind and heart. It's an attitude that you decide to adopt and then make a commitment to maintaining long term.

While consistently behaving in a professional manner takes effort, you shouldn't brag publicly about your professionalism. It reminds me of a Biblical principle that says someone who is fasting or making some sacrifice on behalf of God should not try to draw attention to it. Such a person should go about living normally. So too should professionals. Just adopt good professional behavior and let your actions speak volumes about who you truly are.

Be energetic and enthusiastic. Perpetual professionals show confidence in themselves and the people around them. Optimism is important too. Human beings like to follow optimistic leaders. Those who lead optimistically make our lives more exciting and give us hope for the future.

Finally, a true professional sees no need to apologize for what he or she has not yet accomplished. This is a common problem among young professionals who are still developing their confidence levels. Some people feel intimidated when they are around other professionals whom they perceive to be more successful. You can't undo your past. You can only affect the present and future. Instead of being apologetic about your personal history, commit yourself to shaping your future.

From "Don't Know You" to "Can't Live Without You"

MANY OF THE SELF-MARKETING TIPS IN THIS BOOK ARE DESIGNED TO help you build name recognition and thus facilitate opportunity. A self marketer must be as savvy as a politician running for office and must think of himself or herself as a business of one. This leads to new clients, business opportunities or greater success in selling whatever product or service your company produces.

These are fantastic reasons to engage in self marketing, but let's cut to the chase: Many self marketers are doing so to further their own careers. Specifically, they want to set themselves up for better, higher paying jobs.

Finding a bigger job is a perfect reason to promote yourself in public, but to fully exploit your potential, you need to possess a very important ability: how to move prospective employers from a point in time when they don't know you to another point in time when they believe they can't live without you.

> Believe me,
> if the hiring
> manager didn't
> have a problem,
> he or she wouldn't
> be going through
> the search process.

In a nutshell, that is the key to job searching – finding a way to move the would-be boss from don't-know-you to can't-live-without-you. Yes, it's somewhat manipulative, but it's really no different than any marketing campaign that a company or politician would undertake. Although the process of moving an employer from don't-know-you to can't-live-without-you is not easy per se, it's not nearly as difficult as you might think.

A successful job searcher uses every part of the process – from the cover letter to the final interview – to convince the employer that he or she is the solution to the employer's problem, whatever that may be. If you can show how you are the solution to the problem, you have taken the first major step in moving the employer from don't-know-you to can't-live-without-you.

Every hiring manager has a problem. A great employee could have resigned and defected to a direct competitor. Perhaps someone was fired, which has left psychological scars and social division in the department. The hiring manager could be under tremendous pressure from higher-ups to produce more while spending less. Whatever the particular problem may be, a hiring manager always has one.

Believe me, if the hiring manager didn't have a problem, he or she wouldn't be going through the search process. Finding, hiring and orienting new employees is an expensive, time-consuming pain in the backside. As a man who has hired hundreds of employees over the years, I can attest that conducting a candidate search is a costly endeavor. It takes time away from the activities that directly make the company money. Successful people only spend time on tasks that further their goals. They conduct candidate searches only because they have problems that need solutions.

The successful candidate, the one who moves the hiring manager from don't-know-you to can't-live-without-you, is the one who shows that he or she is the solution to the hiring manager's problem. Later on, we'll discuss how to prove you are the solution by using the various steps of the job search process, but for now suffice it to say, you must prove you are a solution.

The second requirement in moving the hiring manager from don't-know-you to can't-live-without-you is to build rapport with the manager. You want the prospective boss to like you. It is common for job searchers to overlook this. We all know that managers and subordinates aren't supposed to be chummy buddies, but you still want to work with someone with whom you can get along.

Nobody hires people they don't like. Sure, a hiring manager may grow to dislike an employee over the course of time, but in the beginning, nobody hires a person they dislike. It makes sense if you think about it. We spend more waking hours with our colleagues than we do with our families and friends. You might as well spend those hours with people who are pleasant to be around. That's why the successful candidate builds rapport with the hiring manager in addition to proving that he or she is the solution to the problem.

Assuming you are technically competent or have the transferable skills necessary to do a job, you just have to do two things to convince the hiring manager that he can't live without you: build rapport and prove you are the solution to his problem. Candidates who accomplish this can simply wait for the process to play itself out.

Once the hiring manager realizes how valuable you would be to him or her, the rest of the process kind of takes care of itself. Hiring managers go through a mental and emotional roller coaster from the time a job comes open to the time they make decisions. At most large companies, they must also go through several layers of bureaucratic red tape: requisition a job, redesign the job description any time there is a vacancy, deal with the human resources department, sort through countless resumés and so it goes.

After jumping through all the bureaucratic hoops, a hiring manager comes to a point where he or she psychologically commits to the one top candidate. When this happens, the tables turn and the candidate has all the power.

MANIPULATING THE HIRING MANAGER

I'll never forget the first time I hired a professional-level staff person. I was the newly appointed director of enrollment management at a small private college, and I was putting my team together. I had already hired a couple of clerical staff members and several part-time employees in my career, but this was going to be the first time I hired someone for a salaried position that required a bachelor degree. I was excited as soon as the vacancy opened, because I would be able to get rid of the existing person who was carrying too much baggage and replace him with my own, hand-picked person.

We received about a hundred resumés for the position. We whittled the stack down to seven, whom we interviewed by phone. Four candidates came to the office for in-person interviews. One guy stood out. He was fresh out of college, but was extraordinarily talented and was Mr. Everything on campus. This position required someone who was outgoing and had good marketing skills. He was all that and more. He appeared to be just the right fit.

I brought my top candidate back for an additional interview. On the second visit, he met with me, then with the vice president, then the president, then a committee of my colleagues from other campus offices. He even met the gatekeepers in human resources. He impressed everyone. We all agreed that he was the top choice. My boss and I talked with HR and determined an offering salary. I was told to go and give him the offer.

I was so excited. I hurried downstairs to my office, closed the door, pulled out his file and picked up the phone. Suddenly, I was short of breath, and I realized my heart was beating fast. Afraid of sounding "nervous" on the phone, I hung up the receiver.

It's kind of embarrassing to say, but that nervous feeling reminded me of being back in high school, feeling nervous about calling a girl. I can remember, as a kid, calling girls I liked and being so nervous that I would hang up the phone really fast, or the phone would start ringing, and I'd be thinking, "Please let the answering machine pick up!"

I must say, it felt weird to have such a feeling when I was calling some dude to offer him a job. What was wrong with me? I asked myself. "He should be nervous that I won't call!"

It bothered me that I was so anxious about this, but there was a very good reason for it: I was afraid he would turn me down. After I psychologically invested in him, I didn't want to hear him say, "No thanks." Over the course of the long candidate search, this guy moved me from a point where I didn't know him to a point where I thought I couldn't live without him. He did what successful candidates do: He manipulated the hiring manager's emotions to his benefit.

When I finally took a deep breath, calmed down and called him, he said he needed to think about it. He took two days, asked for more money, which we gave him, and started two weeks later. He turned out to be a great member of my team, and the experience in selecting and hiring him taught me a valuable lesson that has benefited my career ever since.

STEPS TO SUCCESS

A hiring manager must go through about 25 steps to replace a former employee with a new one. These steps sometimes stretch over several months. Despite all that must happen to bring a new employee on board, there are essentially only two points in the hiring process where a good self marketer builds rapport with the hiring manager and shows that he or she is the solution to the manager's problems. The first is the resumé and the second is the interview.

Resumés

A resumé has one purpose and one purpose only: to get you an interview. A resumé that fails to catch the eye of a reviewer and thus lead to an interview is a flawed resumé. As you write yours, keep this in mind. Ask yourself whether or not the wording and appearance of your resumé is moving you toward an interview.

There is no single "right" way to write a resumé. Numerous format variations are acceptable.

Some job seekers like to summarize their career-long experiences and abilities in a broad, general section at the top. Such a summary typically doesn't connect experiences and abilities to a particular job, but rather it's a macro view of the job seeker's overall career. When I'm reviewing resumés, I never look at summary statements, but I know several managers who do.

You can take a lot of liberties in designing your resumé but avoid the cutesy stuff. Back when I was a college senior, a fraternity brother of mine hired a consultant to help him find a job. She advised him to put his resumé on colorful paper that was bigger than the standard 8.5 x 11 business letter paper. That was bad advice. Patently obvious gimmicks designed to grab attention and "make you stand out in a crowd" are annoying to the reviewer. Such gimmicks could make you look unprofessional – a deadly sin in the job-search game.

While format does not matter, grammar, spelling and punctuation do. Your resumé must be grammatically perfect. There is literally no margin of error with this rule. In this day and age of spell-checking and grammar-checking, there is no excuse for typographical errors and careless grammar.

Serious job-seekers follow the "two-sets-of-eyes rule." Having someone else read and carefully review your resumé lessens the likelihood of an embarrassing mistake. As the writer of the resumé and the person who has lived what's on it, you are too close to the situation to effectively critique it. Another person brings a fresh perspective. Always have someone proofread your resumé.

It is perfectly acceptable for your resumé to be more than a page if you have a number of accomplishments. Accomplished executives often have very lengthy resumés. Some professionals will use a curriculum vita instead of a resumé. Curricula vitae are essentially longer, more in-depth versions of resumés. They often list all the articles or books the person has published as well as presentations and seminars delivered. These are used commonly in academe, medicine, research and by highly successful executives. For most professional positions, a standard one- to two-page resumé will suffice.

Most resumés have an objective statement at the top. I don't believe these are necessary, but most people include them. I never read them. They don't tell me anything, because usually they are merely a bunch of jargon-like words that really don't say anything. If you are going to write an objective statement, make it something more than the clichés most people use.

I'm tired of reading objective statements like this:

"I am seeking a management position in a progressive, forward-thinking financial services firm, where I can enjoy a challenge and grow as a professional."

This is a typical objective statement, but it's also a flawed one. Why? There are a couple reasons. For starters, it really doesn't communicate anything substantive, and it's full of clichés. Everyone thinks their company is forward-thinking. "Enjoy a challenge" and "grow as a professional" are overused phrases.

Second, the writer of this objective statement focuses solely on himself – he appears to be self-centered and self-absorbed. If I read this as a hiring manager, I'm left wondering what this person would do for me and my company. Since job-searching is a form of marketing, everything in the resumé, including the objective statement, needs to be written with marketing in mind.

When you are advertising a product, you always focus on how it will benefit the consumer. When you are advertising yourself as a prospective employee, you must show the customer, in this case the hiring manager, how the product, in this case, you, would be beneficial. Hiring managers aren't going to hire you just so they can give you a challenge and help you grow. They're going to hire you if you can make them look good, make their department more efficient and help the company make more money.

In that spirit, it would be far better to write an objective statement like this:

"I am interested in using my ability to relate to customers, my strong understanding of financial practices and my highly developed supervisory skills to obtain a management position in a financial services firm, allowing me to exceed customer expectations while helping the company be more efficient and profitable."

Market the benefit to the consumer, not yourself.

In order to save time, many job seekers now submit resumés electronically. This is completely acceptable. In fact, some employers will only accept resumés that arrive over the Internet. You have to be careful to maintain professionalism, however, while conducting your job search online.

Many online career listing services allow you to respond quickly. At the click of a mouse, you can forward your resumé to any company listing a job opportunity. Unfortunately, the clean formatting of your resumé is sometimes distorted when you do this. I get enough resumés through online career listing services that I understand this and don't hold it against anyone. However, I am so impressed when a professional goes to the trouble of mailing a hard copy on formal paper in addition to the electronic submission.

To make sure your resumé is transmitted in your carefully designed format, email it as an attachment. Just be sure to send the attachment in a professional form. Never send a resumé in a raw format, such as Microsoft Word. Instead, convert professional documents into PDFs. In this format, you don't have to worry about someone accidentally or deliberately changing your resumé or copying and pasting something into or out of it. It's not professional when someone sends a Word document where I can see squiggly lines under words the program doesn't recognize. A PDF conveys a touch of class.

Regardless of the format used, at some point, your resumé should have a chronological listing of everything you have done in your career. Some job applicants incorporate so much creativity in their resumés that it's hard to get a handle on exactly what they have done and when. Ultimately, the reader wants to know the title of each job, the name of the company, the dates of employment and the major responsibilities of that job. Make this as clear and straightforward as possible.

Certain aspects of one's career can cause a resumé dilemma. Many job applicants have "holes" in their careers. They may have stayed home a couple years to raise children or took time off to write the great American novel that unfortunately didn't turn out so great. Whatever the reason, don't succumb to the temptation to cover up these holes. Don't lie about them and don't try to hide them. In the long run, your job search is best served when you are honest.

A dilemma similar to a resumé hole would be a stint at a lesser job – perhaps a person was downsized and, in scrambling for a job, had to take a lower-paying one. This is common. Just go ahead and put the job on your resumé. You draw more attention to a career-reversing job by having a period of unexplained time in your resumé.

Staffing agencies, which hire employees and then contract them out to their client companies, are becoming more and more prominent these days. Even in the professional ranks, many people are working for staffing agencies but spend months or years assigned to a certain company. In this situation, it feels as if you work for the assigned company, but technically, you're an employee of the agency. Staffing agencies provide great career opportunities, and they are a completely legitimate way to lead your career.

When writing their resumés, some staffing agency employees wonder if they should list the staffing agency or the companies to whom they were assigned. My advice is to list both and clearly explain what you did at each assignment (assuming the assignment wasn't just a couple days).

Whether you are dealing with a resumé hole, a career sabbatical or a temporary step backward in your career, honesty is the best answer. Clearly explain what you have done in a truthful manner focusing on the most positive aspects.

The resumé advice discussed so far is quite important, but it's basic, foundational. A resumé is simply a printed self marketing piece, so we now have to focus on how it can be used to move a prospective employer from don't-know-you to can't-live-without-you.

Remember that you convince an employer that he can't live without you by building rapport and showing that you are the solution to the problem. While it's hard to build rapport in a written resumé, it's easy to show how you can be a solution to a problem. Effective resumés use action verbs and strong, descriptive nouns and adjectives.

It's critically important that you use key buzzwords in your resumé as you describe your career experiences. The buzzwords should relate directly to the job you are seeking. To find the right buzzwords, look at the job advertisement and see how it was written. Pull words from that. Look up the company online and see if you can find information about the position or the department in which it is located. There could be some wonderfully descriptive words there. If you already work in the same field, think about the industry buzzwords that are currently in vogue.

Buzzwords are vitally important, because the average hiring manger only spends a few seconds looking at each resumé, at least during the first-round review. As she breezes through the resumés, she's looking for something to jump out – titles, companies and buzzwords.

If I'm hiring a budget analyst, I'm going to be scanning resumés looking for words such as *budget, analysis, planning, strategic, spreadsheet, Excel, zero-based, accounting* and the like. Coming up with buzzwords is not rocket science; in fact, if you know anything about the industry, it should be rather easy. A lot of it is just common sense.

Ultimately, a resumé should be a carefully planned marketing piece that is part of your overall strategic self marketing effort. Spend time on it and customize it for specific jobs. Be honest, but make it a tool that begins to convince the hiring manager that you are the solution to the problem.

Interviews

If you make it through the resumé phase of the hiring process, congratulations! You are now ready for the single most important and difficult part: the interview. There's no doubt that resumés are critically important, but they only exist for one reason – to get you an interview.

Interviews provide the best opportunity for building rapport and proving you are the solution to the hiring manager's problem. Through phone interviews, in-person interviews and second interviews, the relationship between job seeker and hiring manager is forged.

Because so much is riding on them, interviews foster feelings of anxiety in job seekers. The very structure of an interview engenders feelings of discomfort. The interview process is very artificial. It feels unnatural. Think about it: You dress up, go to a strange place, answer probing questions while some seemingly important person (or a committee of them) stares you down, evaluating your every word and movement. You assume you're competing with others, but you never see them and have no idea how you compare to them. The whole process feels like it is stacked in the employer's favor.

> **Because so much is riding on them, interviews foster feelings of anxiety in job seekers.**

It's okay to be a little nervous in an interview, but you don't want it to hamper your performance. Overcoming your anxiety is necessary to gain control in the interview. When you can grab some of the control, it makes you look good and starts you down the path to "can't live without you."

There are a number of things you can do prior to the interview – the night before and the morning of – to make you feel more confident and behave more gracefully.

First, dress professionally. Even if you are interviewing at a famously casual company, you should dress up for the interview. This shows that you are a serious professional and that you value and respect the company with whom you are interviewing.

It is much better to be overdressed than underdressed. As I like to advise my college students, you can wear a business suit to McDonald's and nobody notices you, but if you wear a tank-top and shorts to a five-star restaurant, they'll kick you out. If you show up to a job interview underdressed, you will make a negative impression, and even worse, it could affect your confidence and self-esteem, ruining your chances of getting the job.

Punctuality is another anti-anxiety weapon. Always be a little bit early for an interview. No matter what, you never want to be late. That's a huge red flag to an employer and could immediately disqualify you.

Being early helps your state of mind. There is nothing worse than running late for something as important as an interview, then getting stuck in traffic. I hate that sinking feeling you get, while stuck behind a line of cars in a construction zone, watching helplessly as the seconds tick away on your watch.

If after speeding, weaving through traffic and running an occasional red light, you arrive at the interview site right at the scheduled time, you may feel compelled to run into the building and right into the appropriate office. By the time you get there, your nerves are frayed, you're sweating, you're short of breath and you haven't had a chance to compose yourself.

Arriving early allows you to stop in the restroom to check your hair and straighten your clothing. It gives you time to pop a breath mint and make sure you have your portfolio notebook. You can prevent a great deal of interview-spoiling anxiety by not rushing yourself.

There are some things you as an interviewee can do the day before the interview to increase your effectiveness and dramatically reduce nervousness.

Take some time to study the company and the position. Most companies offer a wealth of information about themselves on the Internet. Corporate websites typically list mission statements, history, executive bios and services offered. Some websites will even include the annual report and descriptions of open jobs. Research the company thoroughly. Also try to research the person who will be interviewing you. Knowledge is power. The more you know, the more confident you will feel. Research also allows you to ask great questions and makes you seem more confident. In this day and age, with so much information at our fingertips, it is inexcusable to be uninformed about a company with which you are interviewing.

This next piece of advice may seem a little obsessive-compulsive, but it is actually a wise idea. Take some time the day before the interview to map out the route you will take. Then, drive that route. This is especially important if you are interviewing in a different city. You'll sleep better the night before the interview, because you already know exactly where you are going. Getting lost, and consequently arriving late, is one less thing you'll have to worry about.

Check your wardrobe the day before the interview. If you don't normally wear business attire to your current job, check to see if you need your suit pressed or dry-cleaned.

Some of your time the night before an interview should be spent reflecting on your career to date. Do a self-assessment. Look over your resumé. I find it amazing that many of the candidates I have interviewed over the years don't seem to know what's on their own resumés. I'll ask them a direct question about something on their resumé, and I'll get a blank stare, at least momentarily. It's probably part nerves, but many people write their resumés months or years before going to an interview. Over the course of time, they kind of forget some of the things that are on there.

As you study your resumé the night before, think about the kinds of questions an interviewer would likely ask about your experiences. Determine how you would answer these questions.

Finally, it's a good idea to spend some quiet time alone visualizing success. Athletes do this before competition, but it works well for job seekers too. Close your eyes and imagine yourself in the interview room. Picture yourself being confident, graceful and knowledgeable. Imagine yourself standing strong, looking great, smiling and shaking hands with everyone you meet. You are impressive. You are professional. You are just the person that company needs to hire. It's good to feel just a tad bit cocky as you drive to the interview location.

The interview advice so far has been about preparation. Now we'll turn our focus to the behaviors and actions you will undertake once you arrive at the interview site.

Keep in mind that you are being watched and evaluated constantly. From the moment you drive within sight of the building where you are interviewing, assume you are being observed. Don't do anything embarrassing. Don't act unprofessionally at any time even when you are sure no one sees you. Don't say anything bad about anyone or anything. Don't say anything "off the record." There's a very good chance that it actually will become part of the record as soon as you leave.

Smart interviewees do not give anyone in the company a reason not to hire them.

Avoid gossip, don't say inappropriate things and never bad-mouth your current employer.

Smart interviewees do not give anyone in the company a reason not to hire them. Think like a politician, and don't say anything that would hurt your chances.

No matter how great it may appear, every single organization is plagued with politics. Anytime you get a plurality of people in one place, politics naturally appear. Political scientist Harold Lasswell was famous for saying, "Politics is who gets what, when and how." Politics is a method for allocating resources and settling conflicts. In any group there are differences of opinion and competition for power, resources and prestige. Therefore, ALL groups are political.

Companies are as political as any organization. A job seeker shouldn't be naïve about this as he arrives at the office building for his interview. The tricky thing is that the interviewee has no way of knowing just what the company's political atmosphere is like (although if you're at all perceptive, you'll start to pick up on it immediately).

That's why you don't say or do stupid things that could make you a victim of internal politics. At any point during your interview visit to the company, you could end up talking to someone who: 1. hates your prospective boss; 2. was the best friend of the previous job holder, who was fired; 3. does not think the job you are trying to get is necessary; 4. tried to get the job you are applying for but was denied. Given all the potential land mines lying around in any company, don't do anything that would make it easier for you to blow up.

Try to make a positive impression with everyone you meet during an interview, including the secretaries or lower-ranking management staff. It is common for nervous interviewees to be so focused on impressing the prospective employer that they end up being rudely dismissive of the receptionists, administrative assistants or other staff members.

Be friendly and respectful of everyone you meet. Any one of the lower-ranking employees could destroy your chances of landing the job. If a lower-level staff member feels disrespected, he or she will likely go into the boss's office after you leave and express strong opinions as to why you should not be hired. Being nice to those who are seemingly powerless just might be what it takes to get the powerful decision maker to choose you.

It is not the best candidate who gets the job; it's the best fit. Selecting a new employee based on resumés and interviews is a subjective process. If it were objective, you would have everyone take a standardized test and then give each person a six-month trial run. Whoever does best on some combined performance score would get the job permanently. Obviously, this is not practical, so we are stuck with the current system.

Given that selections are subjective, you need to manipulate the process to your favor. As indicated earlier, you must move the hiring manager from don't-know-you to can't-live-without-you by building rapport and convincing him that you are the solution to his problems. Interviews are the best time to do this.

Building rapport with the would-be boss is easy if you have the right attitude. Just smiling, being friendly, energetic and attentive is a big part of it. Listen carefully anytime the interviewer explains the job, department or company. Any person loves it when someone else is really listening.

You will build deeper rapport by engaging in conversation with the hiring manager instead of simply answering questions. Much of the interview will be structured, but I am always impressed with candidates who engage me in conversation. It's easy to do. As you answer the interviewer's questions, periodically ask a question back. Start some dialogue going, and you will soon become someone the boss likes.

Questions are critically important to building rapport and also for establishing your credibility. The interviewer is not the only question asker. Interviewees should ask almost as many. Asking questions makes you look interested and enthused. It shows that you are a leader. It also helps you psychologically, because whoever is asking questions is in control at that moment.

Most interviewers will offer you an opportunity to ask questions at the end of the interview. No matter how much the interviewer has explained to you prior to that, always, always, always ask something at this time. If you have nothing to ask, you will appear to lack curiosity and will come across as shallow and dull. As I indicated earlier, don't wait to be invited to ask questions. Toss a couple at the prospective boss as the interview is going along.

Personal questions are ideal rapport-building tools. To get the would-be boss to like you, ask him about himself. We all have egos, and we're all flattered when someone wants to know about us. I don't know about you, but I'll admit that I am one of my favorite subjects. So it is with most people. Ask the interviewer about his career and how he made it to his current position. Ask him about his future goals. Ask him how he has built his department to its current level of success. If you do this with sincerity, it will go a long way to getting the boss to like you.

Successful candidates use every point in the hiring process to build rapport. The same holds true when proving you are the solution to the hiring manager's problem. There are a number of ways to do this. First, answer each of the interview questions in such a way to show that your background would be of benefit to the new job. Just as you used key phrases and buzzwords in your resumé, so too should you in the interview.

Paint a picture with your words, showing how you could come in, get work done and solve problems. In describing your education, previous employment and civic involvement experiences, give examples of how you solved problems and made your superiors look good. Talk about how you like to be a loyal team member with the boss. Describe how you like to work side-by-side with your boss, together solving problems and accomplishing the company's goals.

When answering questions, show that your previous skills and experiences are transferable to the new job. Every skill is a transferable skill. This is important to remember, because many job seekers start to have doubts about their qualifications when interviewing for a new job. Don't let yourself think this, because it will manifest itself into a confidence deficit, which will thus affect your performance in the interview.

Skills are skills and most jobs use the same basic ones. You have to learn new procedures, subject matter and jargon in a new job, but the basic skills remain static. If you are interviewing for a job in a completely different field, it's a good idea to stress this to the interviewer. Let her know how confident you are in the transferability of your skills.

As soon as you return home after an interview, sit down at your computer and write and send a thank-you note. In writing it, make sure you reiterate some of the strongest arguments in your favor.

A STRATEGIC FRAME OF MIND

Landing a new job requires strategic planning and the right attitude. It is easy to become overwhelmed and stressed with the job-search process.

Job searching is a game. It's a high-stakes game, but a game nonetheless. Try to enjoy the process while it's going on and use it as an opportunity to learn and better yourself. You know you will eventually get a new job in the end. After all, look at all the morons you know who have landed good jobs. It's just a matter of time before the right job will land in your lap.

To be more successful, take some time at the beginning to map out a strategy for your job search. Just as self marketing requires a personal strategic marketing plan, you also need a strategic plan when kicking off a job search. In chapter 12, we discussed several classic marketing techniques you can use to build your personal brand. Those same techniques apply to job searching.

A job search is like a multi-media marketing campaign. You, a talented hard-working professional, are the product. You need to identify a target audience, which would be the companies for which you would like to work. You need a communication plan – informal networking, formal networking, responding to employment ads. Sending resumés is analogous to a company sending direct mail in that you must send quite a few of them before you get a single interview. Assume a low response rate. If your response rate is high, consider it a pleasant surprise.

A professional who designs a sound job-search plan, adopts a positive attitude and patiently carries out the plan one step at a time will ultimately land a great job. Don't get discouraged if it takes longer than you wish. Not every marketing plan generates massive sales right away. You have to stick with a marketing plan, fine-tuning it as you go along, giving it time to set roots. A job search is just one type of campaign.

Ultimately, you are in charge of the job search process. You and only you control your career. You are a talented, hard-working professional who brings something special to any job you take. You will make a new employer very happy some day. With the right attitude, commitment and good planning, you will soon move your future boss from don't-know-you to can't-live-without-you.

CHAPTER EIGHTEEN

Take Your Foot Out of Your Mouth and Roll with the Punches

A FRIEND OF MINE, JON, RECENTLY WAS INVITED TO A BLACK-TIE CHARITY dinner held under the rotunda of the state capitol building. He was seated next to an engaging gentleman with whom he struck up an interesting conversation. After several minutes of talking, Jon asked the man, "So, what do you do?"

The man looked a little surprised. "I run this place," he said with a smile. "I'm the Governor."

Needless to say, it was an embarrassing moment for a respected businessman like Jon. Other people at the table got quite a laugh, however. The Governor was in the middle of a political campaign, and his face was plastered all over television and the newspapers. Gracefully, Jon laughed it off and just chalked it up as one of life's funny moments.

The point of the story is that self marketing isn't easy, and it doesn't always turn out the way you want. When you go out into the world to network and build a name for yourself, you are taking a risk: You could make a mistake. You could embarrass yourself. You could offend some-one unintentionally.

Self marketers must be vigilant, trying to avoid sticking the proverbial foot in the mouth. Yet, no matter how careful you are, and no matter how much social grace God has bestowed upon you, chances are you will have embarrassing moments like Jon's every now and then.

Murphy's Law says, "Anything that can go wrong will go wrong." Although that is excessively pessimistic, it often rings true. Assume that Murphy's Law will occasionally bite you on your backside. What separates the successful people from everyone else is their ability to brush off social setbacks and proceed as if nothing really happened.

As Abraham Lincoln said, "My great concern is not whether you have failed, but whether you are content with your failure." That's a great statement for self marketing professionals to ponder.

Regardless of how intimidating a networking opportunity may appear to be, don't hold back. Don't deny yourself the opportunity to make a sale, further your career or build your business simply because you fear embarrassment or failure.

RICE PILAF AND THE WORST INTERVIEW EVER

In 1994, when I was working at the College of Santa Fe in New Mexico, I decided I wanted to return to my hometown of Omaha. I start-ed sending resumés to various employers and eventually landed an inter-view in nearby Lincoln at the University of Nebraska, my alma mater.

I found out about the interview while I was recruiting prospective students in Boston. Because this particular office of the university was short-staffed, they were in dire need of a new person. The director wanted to fast-track the hiring process, which meant he wanted to meet with me right away. I made arrangements for a flight leaving the Albuquerque airport the morning after I was scheduled to return.

As I left Boston for my cross-continental trip, my stomach started to feel uncomfortable. By the time we stopped for a layover at O'Hare in Chicago, I was feeling downright nauseous. As luck would have it, a series of thunderstorms and tornadoes over the southern plains backed-up air traffic nationwide, delaying my departure from Chicago by several hours.

By the time I landed in Albuquerque, it was after midnight, many hours later than my scheduled arrival. Not only was I sicker than a dog, my flight to Omaha the next morning was scheduled to leave at 4:50 a.m. Instead of driving all the way back to Santa Fe, I got a room near the airport for a few hours sleep. Unfortunately, instead of sleeping, I spent most of the night in the bathroom.

Being an ambitious guy, I forced myself into the shower at 3 a.m., managed to get back to the terminal and got on that plane. By the time I landed in Omaha, I was even worse off. As I drove the 60-mile stretch from Omaha to Lincoln, fighting dizziness and nausea, it occurred to me that maybe I should have rescheduled. Oh well, I told myself, it was too late.

I arrived at the interview site. The director greeted me and took me into a conference room for an interview with an eight-person committee. As luck would have it, they seated me at the head of the table in front of a big window where the sun shone through, beating on my body like a radioactive beam of death.

At the very beginning of the interview, adrenaline allowed me to forget how sick I was. Unfortunately, I was soon reminded. It was so hot in there that drops of sweat started forming on my forehead and dripped down my face. After a few minutes, sweat was soaking through my shirt.

Then the nausea came back. As I was answering questions for this committee, I was physically forcing myself not to get sick. Committee members were looking at me with strange expressions – that mixture of pity and concern. At one point, I was debating in my head whether it would be worse to suddenly jump out of my seat and sprint to the bathroom or just throw up all over the conference table.

Although it was humiliating, I mercifully made it through the committee interview without getting sick. The director then told me another three or four people were scheduled to interview with me over lunch.

We walked to an exclusive restaurant, one of those clubs where you must have a membership to be admitted – nice place.

Problems continued at the lunch meeting. To reduce the risk of a very embarrassing situation, I made sure not to let any food actually enter my stomach. To make it seem less obvious, I played around with my food while I talked and answered questions.

Now, when I talk, I have a tendency to gesture quite a bit with my hands. I don't know how exactly it happened, but apparently the tines of my fork were under the rice pilaf while the handle was hanging off my plate. Somehow, my hand hit the edge of the fork, converting it to a food catapult.

Rice pilaf flew up into the air like a fountain, covering everyone at the table. People were literally picking rice and bits of chopped veggies out of their hair and brushing it off their clothing. At the end of lunch, as we all stood up, rice pilaf fell from everyone's laps. It was an unmitigated disaster. As he walked me out of the club, the would-be boss, told me, "We'll be in touch."

I left the interview, knowing I wouldn't get the job. What made it worse was that I humiliated myself in front of so many people at my alma mater.

Sitting in my Santa Fe office a couple days later, my phone rang. It was the director calling from Lincoln. "Jeff, we offered the job to someone else," he said. "The committee just didn't feel comfortable with you." I wanted to tell him that I didn't feel too comfortable either.

I was disappointed. The job would have been a fun one, and I would have been good at it. I wasn't depressed too long, however. I was offered another interview later that week with Clarkson College. In a twist of irony, one of the interviewers embarrassed himself during the Clarkson College interview. As the vice president took a bite out of his sandwich, the turkey, lettuce and tomato squirted out onto the table.

The Clarkson job turned out to be a tremendous opportunity. It led to internal promotions to director of enrollment management and dean of student services. As I look back on that awful rice pilaf interview in

Lincoln, I thank God I didn't get that job. The one I did get truly launched my career.

I often speak to college students about career success, and I always tell this story. It generates a lot of laughs, but that's not why I tell it. I hope my experience makes others more comfortable in their own job-searching experiences. It is highly unlikely that anyone would ever have such an embarrassing interview experience.

It is also a great story for self marketers to ponder. Every time you go out in public, you do run the risk of embarrassing yourself. It's worth the risk! To get ahead, you have to stick your neck out and take chances. You can't expect to make a big difference in the world hiding in your closet.

What's so liberating about my rice pilaf story is that no matter how embarrassing a self marketing screw-up might be, another, perhaps better, opportunity is always lurking around the corner. Even if the worst-case scenarios happen, you can bounce back. As they say, tomorrow is another day.

ALL DRESSED UP FOR NOTHING

Sometimes you get all dressed up and nothing happens. That's another self-marketing obstacle that requires you to roll with the punches. As any professional can attest, sometimes you put on your best suit to meet a big-time prospective client who cancels on you at the last minute.

Over the years, I have had several lunch appointments that didn't materialize. After 20 minutes of sitting by yourself in a restaurant, you come to the realization that you've been stood up.

On a few occasions, I've arrived at a venue to give a speech only to find that a grand total of six people have shown up. Few feelings are as underwhelming as giving a speech in a room big enough for a hundred but occupied by only six. As deflating as that situation is, you have to give them your "A" game. The people who did show up expect a nice show, plus you never know: One of them could be the source of a great opportunity.

The point is this: Ambitious self marketers are sometimes left holding the bag. It is tempting to become bitter, resentful or passive-aggressive in such situations. It is okay to feel that way but don't act that way. Good self marketers are forgiving of others. The next time you see a person who stood you up, tell them it's okay and simply reschedule. Successful self marketers are persistent. No matter what happens, they just keep going and going.

Life is a series of peaks and valleys. Although it would be nice if we could spend our entire lives on the mountaintops, that's just not reality. For every moment you enjoy at the mountaintop, you have to invest some time down in the valley. Keep your chin up when you're scraping the bottom of the valley, because it is only a matter of time before you are back on top.

As is the case with a lot of things in life, self marketers have to expect the unexpected. If you're willing to roll with the punches and not let yourself get too down, you have the right attitude.

CHAPTER NINETEEN

Tons of Room at the Top: The Attitude and Altitude of Success

PSYCHOLOGIST ABRAHAM MASLOW CHANGED THE SOCIAL SCIENCES FOR-
ever when he developed his hierarchy of personal needs. Maslow
argued that in order for a person to achieve greatness, or full
potential, he must have certain needs met. The needs can be ranked or
organized into a hierarchical pyramid.

At the base of the pyramid are the very basic needs, called "physiological"
needs, which are required for a human being to stay alive. Among these
needs are food, water, air, shelter, sleep, pain avoidance and sexuality.

Once you have satisfied these basic needs, Maslow believes you can
progress to the next level of the hierarchy: safety and security needs.
These include stability, safety and security. The third ranking, social
needs, includes companionship, affection and friendship. This is
sometimes referred to as the "love-and-belonging" level. Because of
these needs, we are motivated to marry, start a family or join a club. It's
the tribal instinct that all cultures share.

Once the three lowest levels are met, a person then has the luxury of operating at higher levels. The fourth ranking includes the esteem needs. These include ego, self-esteem, the need for recognition and the desire to achieve a lofty status in life. Feelings such as confidence, competence, achievement, mastery, independence, and freedom are implied at this level.

Finally, if a person has satisfied all of the first four levels, he or she is ready to pursue self-actualization, the pinnacle of human existence, according to Maslow. Self-actualized people pursue intellectual curiosities. They are focused on personal growth, achievement and advancement. They constantly seek new challenges and although they thoroughly enjoy their victories, the joy of success only motivates them to conquer something grander.

Most American professionals reach a plateau at the fourth level. That's a good place to be, but they're missing out on something more. They are denying themselves the joy of self-actualization. Maslow claimed that true self-actualization is very rare and that no more than two percent of the world's population ever reaches it.

Don't deny yourself the heady experience of self-actualization. It takes work, dedication, and deliberate planning, but almost any American professional, especially given the rich opportunity and abundance of resources in this country, can reach the hierarchical peak of the pyramid.

Although achieving self-actualization isn't easy, and it doesn't happen overnight, there is a clear path to it. As you contemplate how you can become self-actualized, or perhaps *more* self-actualized, there are several encouraging things to consider.

First, you have total control of the process. You have the freedom and the right to be self-actualized. You don't have to ask permission, and you don't have to wait for someone else to do it for you.

Second, there's no limit to the number of people who can enjoy operating at the peak of human existence. As British Prime Minister Margaret Thatcher said, "People think that at the top there isn't much room. They tend to think of it as an Everest. My message is that there is tons of room at the top."

Essentially, self-actualization is what this book is all about. Why bother going to the trouble of marketing yourself if not for some meaningful goal? Self marketing is hard work, it's time consuming, and depending on which activities you choose to engage in, it can be expensive. You might as well parlay your self marketing efforts into something wonderful.

The message of this chapter is intended to be a liberating one. Self-actualization, or however else you may define success, is always within your grasp. You can manufacture it out of seemingly nothing. To reach Maslow's pinnacle, you need to adopt certain behaviors and beliefs and make them part of your daily life. You have total control of your life. Success starts with you and ends with you.

INDIVIDUALISM

Rugged individualism is a distinct part of American culture. It is a liberating, empowering philosophy that has played a highly significant role in the nation's success. A philosophical respect for the individual has allowed the evolution of our capitalist society, which has generated the greatest and most widely dispersed wealth the world has ever known.

Success starts with you and ends with you.

In America, great opportunity is laid before individual human beings, but so too is great responsibility. Anyone in this country, no matter how lowly they may have started, can rise to great heights. Our history is full of examples.

As a nation of individualists, we believe in putting power in each person's hands. Instead of having government-controlled businesses, services and media, we allow these important social institutions to be owned by individual people, most of whom are motivated by profit. We have the freedom to choose any occupation. We can worship any way we like. We can move to any city within this country without asking permission. All of these liberties are rooted in the philosophy of individualism.

Totalitarianism, or forced collectivism, is the opposite of individualism. When individuals are forced to become part a group against their wishes, it breaks the individual's spirit, thus dampening innovation, motivation, creativity and ultimately happiness. As the economic philosopher John Stuart Mill said, "Whatever crushes individuality is despotism, no matter what name it is called." I could not agree more.

Without individualism, self-actualization is impossible. In order to reach the pinnacle of your own human existence, you need freedom, unrestrained opportunity to pursue your dreams. Maintaining and advancing the rights of the individual is critically important.

Unfortunately, many emerging aspects of American culture are anti-individual and thus threaten our continued prosperity. Each of us must take responsibility to maintain the sanctity of individualism in our society. We do that by insisting on individual rights and opposing the insidious forces of collectivism, excessive political correctness, and social group-think.

Individualists don't allow themselves to be swept up in the temporary passions of popular culture. They are not easily influenced by the media. They transcend superficiality. They do not easily succumb to hyped-up fears. Individualists think rationally, use the resources at their disposal and proceed forward with the attitude of success. When others express doubt and wring their hands in worry, successful individualists hunker down and do what it takes to get the job done.

To succeed, to conquer your fears and realize your dreams, you must be an individualist. In no way does this mean that you shirk your responsibility to serve and care for others. It does mean that you set your own dreams and take full responsibility for your actions. Successful individualists acknowledge that they are in total control of their personal decision-making and take total accountability for their actions.

VICTIMHOOD AND THE BLAME GAME

Unfortunately, healthy individualism is under assault. Too many people in our society have become dependent on government or some other institution instead of taking responsibility for themselves. It has become easy to blame others for our failings or problems. Victimhood has become in vogue over the past couple decades.

American culture is now inundated with victimhood. Television feasts on it. Turn on any daytime talk show, and you will see the glorification of victimhood. Listen to the guests on these shows, and you will hear everyone blamed for their miserable lives – everyone, that is, except for themselves.

We can see evidence of rampant victimhood when something terrible happens, especially when one bad event hurts a lot of people at one time. Our culture's creeping dependence and philosophical embracing of victimhood often paralyzes us. Many years ago, when a terrible flood, earthquake or hurricane would hit, the affected people would band together, take responsibility for their safety, and work hard to rebuild what was lost.

Disturbingly, during recent disasters, such as Hurricane Katrina and others, the first impulse is to gaze helplessly at government. Because of the decline of individualism and the rise of collective dependence, too many Americans see no choice but to be victims. When something goes bad, victims spend their energy blaming others for failing them instead of finding and pursing their own solutions.

I am here to tell you that victimhood and blaming form the single fastest route to failure. Anyone who thinks like a victim and blames others for his shortcomings is so likely to fail, that it's almost guaranteed.

To avoid the victimhood trap, remember three words: responsibility, authority and accountability.

Each person has "responsibility" for himself or herself. Nobody else does. While this is an obligation, it is also a blessing and a great empowerment. Within moral and legal parameters, you decide what you will do, how you will do it and when. Fortunately, you have the "authority" to carry out your responsibility. You have the right and the permission to do what you wish. Finally, you are "accountable" for your actions. Just because you have the right to do something doesn't mean you are immune from any possible consequences.

Given the power of these three words, successful people never blame others for their failures nor do they give away credit for their successes.

A college student may have a learning disability, a foreign professor with a thick accent and a lot of distractions in his personal life, yet there is no excuse for failing the exam. If he does fail, he must look at himself and find a different solution. If you are late for a meeting, it doesn't matter that you got stuck behind a parked train at a railroad crossing. It's your fault for not leaving earlier or taking a different route. Successful people don't make excuses. They accept the blame and fix the problem, so it doesn't happen again.

On the other hand, successful people accept accolades when appropriate. I am certainly not implying that you should be a boasting, egotistical blowhard. I am saying, however, that successful people realize when they do well and know why they do well. If a student gets an "A" on an exam, it happened because she went to class and studied. If a businessman lands a big client, it happened because he had a good product, researched the client and gave a great presentation. Granted, you may have been blessed with a lot of God-given talent, but God expects you to make use of that talent. You are the one who does the work, so you are responsible for the outcome, good or bad.

For successful people, there is no such thing as luck. There is no such thing as fate. They reach their success by taking their talents and making something out of them while remembering "responsibility, authority, accountability."

TAKE THE INITIATIVE

One of the greatest Americans of all time, Benjamin Franklin, advised: "Plough deep while sluggards sleep." Successful people are always on the move. They get things done when they need to be done. Successful people are not afraid to keep working when less accomplished people are taking the day off.

Attaining a state of self-actualization requires you to take the initiative, to be a self-starter. Nobody can do the dirty work required to achieve self-actualization. They can help you, and they can advise you, but it's up to you to actually get there.

Don't wait for opportunities to present themselves to you. That's too passive. It makes you dependent on other people and external conditions you can't control. Instead, be assertive. Go out into the world and make your own opportunities. Create your own luck.

Create your own luck.

Taking the initiative sets you up for career and life success in general. It is also a healthy philosophy for your self marketing plan. Because self marketing takes time and effort and requires you to venture outside your comfort zone, it is tempting to put it off. It is easy to procrastinate.

Some people think they should become richer, smarter or generally more successful before they start self marketing – "I need to develop a good product before I start selling." That's a mistake, because self marketing now helps you fast-track your career. Even as you are learning and growing, you should market yourself constantly along the way.

HEALTHY HABITS

Making a commitment to healthy living is a prerequisite for self-actualization. Those who enjoy long-term success realize that their personal lives must be in order. That means you should care for your mental, physical, emotional, spiritual and financial health as much as for the health of your career. Personal and professional successes are inseparably interwoven.

It is very difficult to be successful at work if your personal life is a mess. If your marriage is dysfunctional, it's hard to focus on high-level career achievement. If you lack a set of core beliefs, you may not be able to create a philosophy of life that guides you to some great achievement. If you are barely keeping your financial head above water, you don't have the financial ability to take on entrepreneurial endeavors. Whatever the problem, you will be more successful in all facets of life if you take care of things at home.

A good attitude does wonders for your success. Think positive thoughts and constantly reinforce yourself in your own mind. As Norman Vincent Peale taught us in his famous book, *The Power of Positive Thinking*, you can cause successful outcomes by forcing yourself to be optimistic. Positive thinking is far healthier than the alternative.

After you adopt a positive attitude, there are several other things you can do that will make you a healthier person.

If you have a faith, I recommend you practice it. Believing in and answering to a higher power has an amazing effect on career success. Prayer, meditation or whatever you choose to call it purges the toxins from your mind and gives you strength and confidence. Faith organizations provide a venue for you to share your talents, giving you a sublime sense of satisfaction. You get to help others, but when you need help, a large group of fellow congregants is ready to give you a hand.

After faith comes family. No matter how ambitious you are, your family should be one of your highest priorities. Do whatever it takes to protect your familial relationships. If things ever get really tough, you want to be able to depend on those who share your blood. Stick up for your family members and look out for their interests. If a family member is in need, drop whatever you are doing and tend to him or her. In the long run you will be far richer if family comes before career.

Close friends are almost as important as family. A long-time friend who truly understands you is worth his or her weight in gold. Put the important people in your life on a pedestal and make them your priority. If you go out of your way to put people first, you will have more business opportunities than you can handle.

Because family and friends are so important, you should adopt an attitude of acceptance. Let them be who they are and love them in spite of all their flaws and weaknesses. Forgive them any time they wrong you. Bite your tongue when you feel like saying something hurtful or insulting to a friend or family member. These relationships are so important that it's foolish to put them at risk over some temporary passion.

While relationship-building contributes to career success, so does physical health. You are more likely to become self-actualized if you exercise and eat right. You don't have to be an obsessive gym rat, but being in shape and consuming the right nutrition gives you more energy and stamina.

Keep your home life organized. Make sure your house is generally clean and tidy. Have a good system for organizing your bills and other important papers. Always put your keys and purse/wallet in the same place. Develop systems and routines for the simple, daily things. If you standardize the little things, they won't become problems that distract you from higher-realm activities. If you run a tight ship at home, you will waste less time – time that could be devoted to important stuff.

Hobbies and recreation are also parts of a healthy life. Having enjoyable stimulation outside work and home recharges your battery and contributes to creative thinking. Hobbies can also be a great way of networking, a critical component of self marketing. Just don't go too hog wild with your hobbies. Some people get so deeply involved in hobbies that they hurt their job performance and drain their bank accounts.

Speaking of bank accounts, personal financial discipline is part of a healthy lifestyle. Just as you need to get your body in shape, you need to shape up your financial condition as well. Philosopher Ralph Waldo Emerson said, "Few people have any next, they live from hand to mouth without a plan, and are always at the end of their line."

A portion of the population has always chosen to live on the edge of the financial abyss, recklessly spending all they have, investing little or nothing. Unfortunately, that portion of the population has been growing rapidly, and it's becoming quite a problem.

A tremendous number of Americans are one missed paycheck away from financial disaster. Our national savings rate recently dipped below zero percent. If it weren't for home equity, the majority of "middle-class" families would have a negative net worth.

Bankruptcies are public record. If you look at the bankruptcy filings in your community, you would probably be shocked at the amount of debt people rack up. Signs of the financial problems are popping up everywhere.

As a commercial real estate professional, I pay close attention to the types of businesses that are leasing space. There have always been a lot of quick-service, check-cashing places in lower socioeconomic parts of town. These are companies that give you an advance on your upcoming paycheck, but you have to pay a ridiculous fee. Now, I'm seeing check-cashing businesses open in new strip malls in some of the most affluent parts of town.

A friend of mine once owned a check-cashing business. Shockingly, many of his regular customers were doctors, lawyers, executives and university professors.

I once worked with a man who made quite a bit of money. Nevertheless, he was up to his eyeballs in debt. Bill collectors called him at work. Colleagues regularly could hear him on the phone in his office arguing with creditors or pleading with one credit card to cover the debt on another credit card. Whether he realized it or not, this was humiliating for him. Co-workers talked behind his back, and none of them respected him.

These financial trouble signs tell me that our country lacks discipline and that our expectations are getting out of whack. Our egos, desires and need to keep up with the Joneses are killing our society financially. We need to embrace the philosophy of delayed gratification. It is simply not prudent to buy whatever you want whenever you want regardless of whether you have the money in your account.

Living a financially reckless life will eventually catch up with you and hurt your career. If you have no savings, you have no "go-to-hell-money," which is the power to walk away from a job when you hate it. A lot of financial debt can prevent you from taking some lower paying job that might actually make you happier. And, in the case of my former co-worker described here, poor financial conditions can be very embarrassing. For every minute you spend worrying and fretting about how you will make ends meet, you are taking away time from your pursuit of self-actualization.

Even though it may put a little crimp in your lifestyle, make sure you are paying down debts and building up your investments. Make financial discipline part of your healthy lifestyle.

COMMITMENT

Former U.S. Secretary of State Colin Powell said, "There are no secrets to success. It is the result of preparation, hard work and learning from failure." While I agree with this statement, it is too simplistic. To achieve real success, or self-actualization, you need to embrace the right attitude. You need to expect success, but you can only do that if you live under the right set of attitudinal rules.

To adopt an attitude of success and pursue self-actualization, you must make a long-term commitment. You can't decide to adopt healthy lifestyle habits and successful attitudes for a short period of time and expect your success to be perpetual. You need to ingrain the attitude of success into the many folds of your brain.

Self-actualization is not a get-rich-quick scheme. Success does not happen overnight. You need to be persistent. You need discipline. You need to make a life-long commitment to the principles described in this chapter. Practicing patience while believing in yourself, acting with healthy assertiveness and working your tail off will eventually lead you to your own understanding of self-actualization.

You:
The Superstar

A S THE CURTAIN ROSE, THE CROWD OF ALMOST 20,000 ERUPTED IN A deafening cacophony of screams and applause. After sitting through two warm-up acts, the musical superstar they had been waiting to see was finally on stage. There he was standing in the spotlight, microphone in hand with his full band backing him up.

To the casual spectator, the superstar on stage appeared to have everything together. He seemed perfect. He had an army of staff members on and off stage, all working to make him look great as he entertained masses of zealous fans.

Rock stars are anomalies. This performer seemed almost like some super being, as if he transcended the normal chains and bonds of human existence, living in some higher realm that the rest of us can only dream about.

When I attended this concert, about three-quarters of this book had been completed, and I was taking a rare night off from writing. As my mind wandered that evening, it's no wonder I started thinking about self marketing. It occurred to me that the superstar on stage was the ultimate self marketer. Everything focused on him, and he parlayed that into millions of dollars, tremendous good will and great influence.

Interestingly, this concert was being filmed for a television show to be aired at a later date. My wife and I made a point to watch the show a couple weeks later. It was one of those programs that documents the making of a concert. It covered everything starting with planning meetings held several months before opening night, through the rehearsals, the travel, the pre-concert rituals and the show itself.

Having attended the concert, we found the documentary quite interesting. Perhaps the most enlightening thing I got out of it was just how fragile the superstar's fame was. When you see a great performer on stage, it's tempting to think it's so easy. I assumed the performer actually did very little, because he had a huge staff leading him the whole way. As a spectator, I just assumed that his image was so big that it had morphed into a self-sustaining beast that fed itself and grew with little or no tending.

Seeing the documentary, it became very clear that the superstar had to do a great deal of hands-on work to keep his fame going. He worked hard. His fame was actually rather thin, in that any letdown in his effort would start to diminish it.

I then remembered that most superstars start out as ordinary people. They work really hard to create something special. They must take risks. They have to surround themselves with the right people in order to make it happen. They need to make good business decisions and then hope for some luck.

I tried to think about what an aspiring music star must go through to make it to the big time. I bet there were times when he felt like giving up. I bet there were times when he felt stupid and awkward perhaps wondering to himself, "What am I doing? I have no business trying to be a professional singer!"

While most of us will never be musical recording sensations, there is something we can learn from a superstar musician's journey from performing in smoke-filled, small-town lounges to standing before tens of thousands of adoring fans in the middle of a football stadium.

In a typical self marketing journey, an ambitious professional tries to go from a little-known entry level worker to a rock star in his or her industry or community. Self marketers strive to become superstars in their own spheres of interest.

Along the way, they encounter challenges, setbacks and, worst of all, self doubt. Creeping self doubt has paralyzed many would-be successful people. There are tons of people in the world with outstanding talent who never accomplish greatness because of self doubt.

If you think you have a good idea, fight through the self doubt.

I will never forget the very first episode of my radio show *Grow Omaha*. As the intro music was playing, I got a feeling of self doubt. With a sick feeling in the pit of my stomach, I turned to my co-host and said, "What the hell are we doing? We have no business being here." He just gave me a nervous smile and a shrug of the shoulder. At that point, the music stopped, and I just started talking.

Now, years later, we have about 10,000 loyal listeners. People tell me it's a brilliant show, something they look forward to each week. It's amazing to think that I almost killed the show several times before it first aired because of creeping self doubt. Thankfully, my colleague and I stayed with our vision and fought off the doubt.

If you strive to do something unique and different as part of your self marketing efforts, be prepared to face self doubt. It's hard not to get a little nervous when you are taking a risk. Self marketing is one of those activities that potentially can bring high rewards but also significant risk. The more you try to market yourself, the more you expose yourself to potential disappointment, failure and embarrassment.

Don't worry about failure. You are better off trying something and failing than not doing it at all. With each disappointment, you learn something that will help you do better next time.

Self marketing is tightly interwoven with leadership, which leads to success. Leaders have to take risks. Leaders keep things afloat no matter what it takes. If you engage in self marketing, you are, by default, exercising leadership skills.

Just remember, the professional world is a high-stakes environment. You are competing with talented people from around the globe. All the competition makes today's marketplace very crowded and noisy. In order to get ahead, you must stand out, be noticed and impress the people around you.

As a professional, you are a business unto yourself. You have a personal brand, which must be perpetually and actively promoted to your target audience. Never forget that, like the politician running for office, you are in a life-long campaign for excellence. A big part of your success or failure will be determined by your ability and willingness to toot your own horn.

I hope this book has inspired you to reach a new level of success in your life-long pursuit of excellence. With a positive attitude, a strong work ethic and the understanding of critical success skills, you have all it takes to achieve greatness. You just need to be willing to tell the world about your accomplishments. Untold opportunities are waiting for you.

You can change your life for the better. It's time to get started.

About the Author

J EFF BEALS'S UNIQUELY DIVERSE CAREER MAKES HIM THE IDEAL PERSON TO reveal and explain the secrets of effective self marketing. As a commercial real estate executive, radio talk show host, newspaper columnist and part-time college professor, Beals understands how to synthesize wide-ranging experiences into one very successful career.

Jeff Beals currently serves as Vice President of Coldwell Banker Commercial World Group, a commercial real estate company, which provides brokerage and property management services to clients in Nebraska and Iowa.

Along with Trenton Magid, he is co-host of *Grow Omaha*, a popular weekly talk show on News Radio 1110 KFAB. Beals writes a bi-weekly column called, "T-Squares & I-Beams" for *The City Weekly* newspaper. Altogether, he has published more than 200 articles in national and local periodicals.

Since 2003, he has served as an adjunct faculty member at the University of Nebraska at Omaha, where he teaches a real estate sales and leasing course in the College of Business Administration.

Before entering the real estate profession in 2001, Beals served as Dean of Student Services and Director of Enrollment Management at

Clarkson College. From 1993 to 1994, he worked as Assistant Director of Admissions at The College of Santa Fe in New Mexico.

Beals holds a master of arts degree in political science and a bachelor of journalism degree in news-editorial both from the University of Nebraska-Lincoln. In addition to his active career, Beals finds time to stay involved in his community and his career field. He lives with his wife, Stephanie, and son, Jack, in Omaha, Nebraska.

More Self Marketing Resources

Additional Copies

Contact Keynote Publishing if you would like additional copies of *Self Marketing Power: Branding Yourself as a Business of One*. The book is also available in other formats: E-book or as an audio recording (coming soon) on compact disc.

Great Gift Idea

Self Marketing Power makes a great gift for professionals, executives, entrepreneurs, salespeople and college students. Consider *Self Marketing Power* as a gift for anyone you know who wants to achieve more, do more business and go farther in life.

Speeches & Seminars

Jeff Beals, author of *Self Marketing Power,* delivers presentations on self marketing to a wide variety of audiences nationwide. These presentations are energetic, humorous and packed full of valuable information. Let's discuss the possibility of a presentation for your organization!

To order copies, additional items
or to book a speaking engagement, go to:

www.selfmarketingpower.com

You can also contact the author at:

Info@selfmarketingpower.com

or

KEYNOTE PUBLISHING, LLC
P.O. Box 540663
Omaha, NE 68154

WHAT OTHERS HAVE SAID
ABOUT JEFF'S PRESENTATIONS

"I have read Jeff's book, Self Marketing Power, *and heard him speak on the same topic. His insights are dead-on. He clearly explains ways that one can achieve growth in his or her career by promoting himself without coming off as brash or self-absorbed. His successful real estate career, radio program, book, and speaking abilities show that he lives what he teaches."*
—**David DeFord, author, speaker, trainer**

"As the keynote speaker at our annual meeting, Jeff Beals held our franchise owners' interest and inspired them to take their business to the next level. Learning to market themselves as 'a brand of one' was the perfect message for them to take back home and include in their marketing plans."
—**Roland Bates, president, National Property Inspections, Inc.**

"Jeff Beals is a compelling speaker and author. His book Self-Marketing Power *is a blueprint for success no matter what your title or field. His strategies for "becoming a celebrity in your own sphere of interest" not only help you become the go-to resource in your network, but is based not on cut-throat competition but on creating mutually beneficial relationships. If you've never heard him speak, make it a priority!"*
—**Susan Baird, freelance writer**

"I enjoyed the talk Jeff Beals gave at the South Dakota Personnel and Placement Association conference. He triggered many new and creative ideas for me, not only in marketing my own skills, but in helping our students to market theirs."
—**Arlene Holmes, career counselor, Black Hills State University**

"Seminars often can be unproductive, however I took a great deal from Jeff's presentation. The most significant piece for me was the notion of becoming an expert at something and using that angle to promote myself. It seems so simple, but I never thought of it in those terms. It was an entertaining, educational and energetic workshop. Jeff truly practices what he preaches."
—**Joe Sova, Paychex, Inc.**

Index

booking speeches, 131, 132
Boston, Massachusetts, 222
brand, 7, 8, 11, 141
    building personal, 11
    promoting, 11
branding, 7, 8, 11, 141
Buffett, Warren, 36, 170
Building Owners and Managers
    Association, 57, 58
building rapport, 81, 92, 217
building relationships, 9-10, 65–67
Bush, H.W., George, 37, 87, 108
business attire, 80, 192–194,
    213-215
business cards, 28, 92, 118, 130, 198
buzzwords, 212, 218

C

C&A Industries, 25
campaign consultants, 33
campaign managers, 33
campaign strategy, 32
career advancement, 11–13, 203–220
Carlyle, Thomas, 23
Carnegie, Dale, 1, 2
CBS Television, 100, 101
celebrity, 13, 33–36, 49
    benefits of, 36, 37
    cost of, 38
cell phone calls, 197, 198
Chambers of Commerce, 45–47
    events, 85
charities, 53
Chicago, Illinois, 34, 117, 155, 222,
    223
children, 51, 52, 154, 211
chit-chat, 86, 124
Churchill, Winston, 128
Cincinnati, Ohio, 35
City Weekly, 15, 20, 114, 117, 243

civic affairs, 16
civic organizations, 4
civility, 28
Clarkson College, 54, 72, 77, 161,
    224
clichés, 110, 209
Coen, Pete, 114
Coldwell Banker Commercial World
    Group, 15, 21, 24, 43, 73, 77,
    102, 109, 130, 243
College of Santa Fe, 222, 244
college recruiting, 153
comfort zone, 22, 43, 233
commitment, 237
Common Cause, 48
common courtesy, 200
common ground, 81, 88
common sense, 148, 149
communicating clearly, 28, 29
communication
    professional, 196–198
community groups, 132
competition, 163, 164
competitive analysis, 143
conferences, 19
conflicts of interest, 70, 71
consistency, 4, 5
Constant Contact, 137
continuing education, 159–167
conventions, 85, 199
core values, 172-177
corporate websites, 214
cost of celebrity, 38
courtesy, 200
creative thinking, 151–158
creativity, 151–158
Cronkite, Walter, 100, 101
cult of celebrity, 33–36
curiosity, 159-163, 218
curriculum vita, 208, 209

T

U

SELF MARKETING POWER
Branding Yourself as a Business of One

O R D E R   F O R M

Customer Name: _____

Date: _____

Shipping Address: _____

City: _____ State: _____ Zip: _____

Telephone: (____) _____ Email: _____

Books = $19.95 X _____ # of copies $ _____
Sales Tax (7% when shipped to Nebraska addresses only) $ _____
Shipping & Handling Media Mail (allow 1-2 weeks)
  or Priority Mail (2-3 days):
USPS Media Mail = $3.00 for 1st book / $1.50 for each additional book $ _____
USPS Priority Mail = $5.00 for 1st book / $2.50 for each additional book $ _____

TOTAL $ _____

Payment Method

❏ Check enclosed made payable to "Keynote Publishing"
❏ VISA   ❏ MasterCard   ❏ American Express   ❏ Discover

Name on Card: _____

Debit or credit? _____

Billing Address: (if different from above)

_____

Account Number: _____

CVV code: _____ Exp. Date: _____
(3 digits on back of card near signature on Visa/MC/Discover – 4 digits on front of American Express)

Cardholder's Signature: _____

Mail order form to:
Keynote Publishing • P.O. Box 540663 • Omaha, NE 68154
www.selfmarketingpower.com

SELF MARKETING POWER
Branding Yourself as a Business of One

Placing Your Order

MAIL order form to:
Keynote Publishing
P.O. Box 540663
Omaha, NE 68154

FAX order form to:
(402) 697-8585

EMAIL your order to:
orders@selfmarketingpower.com

ONLINE orders may be placed at:
www.selfmarketingpower.com

Thank you!

21382714R00174

Made in the USA
Middletown, DE
27 June 2015